Proud-voiced Macedonia

By the same author
LEGACY OF THASOS

Gold-sheathed casket with the radiating star of Macedonia on the lid found within a marble container, Vergina 1978 (by courtesy of Prof. of Arch. at University of Thessaloniki M. Andronikos)

PROUD-VOICED MACEDONIA

A background for King Philip II
and the Royal Burial Ground
at Vergina

JOAN L. WYNNE-THOMAS

Springwood Books

REGENT'S
UNIVERSITY LONDON

© *Joan L. Wynne-Thomas 1979*

First published 1979
by Springwood Books Ltd
49–51 Bedford Row
London WC1V 6RL

Printed in Great Britain by
Butler & Tanner Ltd
Frome and London

ISBN 0 9059 4756 8

To
MANOLIS ANDRONICOS
with admiration and thanks

'*Ithaca has given you the beautiful voyage,*
Without her you would never have taken the road ...'

C. P. CAVAFY

(Translated from the Greek by Rae Dalven)

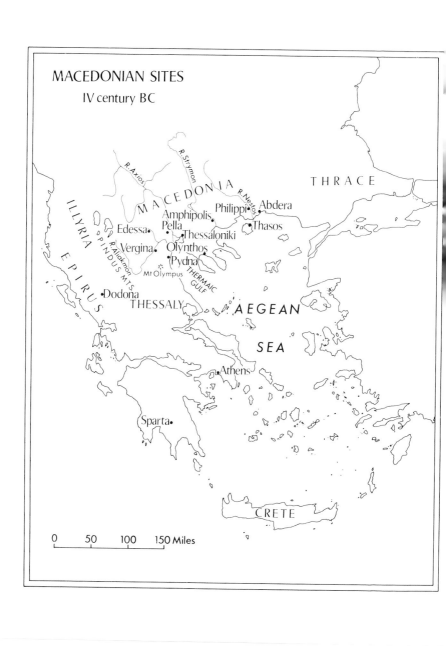

MACEDONIAN SITES
IV century BC

THRACE

R.Axios

R.Strymon

MACEDONIA

R.Nestos

ILLYRIA

PINDUS MTS.

R.Aliakmon

Edessa

Vergina

Pella

Amphipolis

Philippi

Abdera

Thessaloniki

Thasos

Olynthos

Pydna

Mt Olympus

THERMAIC GULF

EPIRUS

Dodona

THESSALY

AEGEAN

SEA

Athens

Sparta

CRETE

0   50   100   150 Miles

Contents

Illustrations

Illustrations

Preface

It is hoped that the sub-title of this book will explain its object, as the actual title is a quotation from a poem in Pausanias' *Guide to Greece* which was written during the second century AD, and is unlikely to be very widely known. Pausanias was a Greek doctor who spent nearly twenty years travelling throughout mainland Greece, during which time he wrote in detail of every Greek city and sanctuary. He also recorded local customs and beliefs, and much historical information.

Few readers can be wholly unaware of the magnificent finds by Professor Manolis Andronicos in 1977 and 1978 of two un-plundered royal tombs in the ancient necropolis at Vergina in Macedonia. These tombs contained considerable treasure, which included a great deal of gold, and it is now almost universally agreed that one of the tombs is that of King Philip II of Macedon.

The personality of Philip is sometimes slightly over-shadowed by that of his more spectacular son – Alexander the Great – but research into Philip's life reveals a remarkable character.

Unfortunately there is comparatively little written history about Macedonia, and therefore archaeological excavation is of para-mount value. The map at the beginning of the book should be of assistance in this study of Philip, as well as of Macedonia, and should enable readers better to understand the geographical background to his life and achievements.

I have received much help in the preparation of this book – the subject of which was suggested to me by one of my many Greek friends – and there are a number of people to whom I owe very real thanks. First of these must be Professor Manolis Andronicos who welcomed me – then a complete stranger – for more than an hour on site at Vergina, in August 1978, only very shortly after he had opened the third tomb. Since then I have had the good fortune not only to hear him lecture in great detail on the royal tombs but to meet him personally on several occasions, when he gave me great help.

Preface

The archaeologist in charge on the site at Abdera was also very helpful, as was the Curator of the museum at Pella who opened it for me on a day when it is normally closed.

Throughout I have had encouragement, interest and practical help on all levels from the Greek Embassy in London, and in particular from Eleni Cubitt without whose help my task would have been far more difficult.

As always my gratitude is due to the Librarians at both the Society of Antiquaries of London, and the Society for the Promotion of Hellenic Studies; and I would also like to place on record my appreciation of the work done for me by Peter Bloodworth and Tony Pocock, the hard-working photographic technicians, who take so much trouble with my films.

Last, but certainly not least, my very grateful thanks are once again due to my publishers, on whose help, advice, interest and courtesy I have come to rely.

JOAN L. WYNNE-THOMAS

Macedonia – Dodona – Bucklebury
1978–1979

Chapter 1

Macedonia – a brief background

Macedonia is a country of considerable contrast, in which high mountain ranges and vast plains are intersected by great rivers. The valleys of the Morava and the Vardar, which together form the Axios, create a central point of entry from Yugoslavia and the Danube basin. Entry is also possible from the Adriatic through Albania and Lake Ochrid, now in Yugoslavia, — the area known as Illyria – although with the present regime in Albania today this is not allowed; and from Bulgaria, through the Struma–Strymon valley to Serrae. To the south there is the extremely narrow Vale of Tempe; and from the east the coastal plain of the lower Nestos to Kavala from Thrace.

The climate of Macedonia is more continental than Mediterranean although very large quantities of olives, vines and fruit are grown, as well as much timber which is suitable for boat-building. The inhabitants are a hardy race, of peasant stock, inured to extremes of both heat and cold. They are a tall people, particularly the men, and in some parts are very good-looking. Work in Macedonia is hard and strenuous. Crop follows crop – cereals, peaches and apricots, vines, olives and tobacco, and all of these except cereals have to be harvested by hand. In certain areas hundreds of thousands of bees are kept, and during the honey season small tents are put up near the hives so that work can continue from dawn till dusk. Transport to and from the colonies of bees is generally on mule-back. Honey was the main sweetener known to ancient peoples, and it had certain religious associations. The bees were thought to gather it from the upper air as well as from the flowers and the pine-trees, and among others Aristotle was a propounder of this theory. Honey was, and still is, used in medicine, cooking and sweatmeats, and is much valued for its preservative qualities.

Macedonia – a brief background

Plato was fed with honey when a baby, and the name of the great god, Zeus, is in some way connected with it.

The north-western plain, with its small towns – Edessa, and Naoussa – is the centre of the fruit industry; being well-watered, it is surprisingly green, even in July and August, when most of the countryside is burnt a yellowish-white. In spring it is extremely beautiful, with mile after mile of fruit blossom, stretching from the little hill town of Edessa to the slopes of Mount Vermion.

Many of the mountains of Macedonia are high, rising in places to more than 7,000 feet; with the great massif of Mount Olympos to the south-east rising to some 10,000 feet.

There are many lakes, some of which are very large, and a long sea coast; and in this area every harbour, and in some places every house, has its fisherman and its boat. Fishing, as in most of Greece, is done by caique, with its accompanying 'gri-gri's'; small boats each containing one fisherman which are towed by the caique, with powerful lights to attract the fish, which are subsequently off-loaded into the caique.

The three-tonged promontory of the Chalkidiki is part of Macedonia, on which is the early Classical site of Olynthos, and also the Mountain of Athos. The most easterly peninsula of the Chalkidiki, the Holy Mountain of Athos is unique in the world. It is a bastion of the Orthodox Christian Church, and contains twenty monasteries, with monks from different countries. Great treasures, holy relics and wonderful libraries are owned by these monasteries. No female creature, animal or human, is allowed on the Holy Mountain, and even young men under the age of twenty-one must be accompanied by their father, or a school-master or professor responsible for them. Only the birds and bees and butterflies, and the myriad of insects are allowed to mate, and breed, and come and go as they will, because it is impossible to stop them. It is, reputedly, a place of high spiritual endeavour, and certainly of great natural beauty, and those who go there say that great peace is to be found upon this holy hill.

The Community on Mount Athos has existed since AD 1060, when the Emperor Constantine IX made an edict forbidding access

to 'any woman, any female, any eunuch, any smooth visage ...'
Today it is no longer necessary to grow a beard. The actual mountain of Athos at the southernmost end of the peninsula is more than 6,000 feet high, and rises sheer from the sea. In pre-Christian days the Holy Mountain was sacred to Zeus.

The island of Thasos is Macedonian, and is only eight kilometres from the eastern Macedonian shore at Keramoti; along this shore is the main tobacco-growing area of northern Greece. Here also is the fifth city of Greece, the charming port of Kavala, from which much of the tobacco is shipped, and to which many caiques bring their catch each morning.

Eastern Macedonia is well-protected from the north by high mountains, and to the east by the river Nestos, although correctly both banks of this beautiful river are in Thrace.

The capital of Macedonia is Thessaloniki, the second city of Greece. It was built comparatively late, and has therefore no remains dating to the Archaic period. Cassander, the son of Antipater, who fought with Alexander the Great in Asia in 324 BC, was responsible for its building. The great fourth century also passed it by; its walls were originally built during the Hellenistic period, and reconstructed by the Romans. There is much of interest in the city of the Byzantine era, and some fine early Christian churches. There is also a most interesting museum which houses much of Macedonia's ancient treasure, including the recent finds from Vergina.

The area of Eastern and Western Macedonia, combined with the Chalkidiki, is greater than that of any other department of Greece, and the present-day population is approximately one and a half million.

Macedonia has been continuously inhabited since the Neolithic period, and a culture is known for it during the Bronze ages which owed little, if anything, to Mycenae.

The Burial Ground at Vergina, which covers an enormous area in the valley of the Aliakmon, contains tombs dating to 1000 BC, the time of the early Iron Age, and burials continued there until

700 BC. This cemetery of tumuli was re-used in the Classical and Hellenistic periods, and it is not impossible that, with time, some Archaic burials will be discovered.

The original history of the royal house of Macedon is best taken from Herodotus, who describes it very fully, and is backed up by Thucydides. Perdiccas I was the first known king of the royal house of the Argeadae. To quote the great historian

> ... Perdiccas won the lordship of the Macedonians in the following way. Three brothers, descendants of Temenos, had been expelled from Argos, and had taken refuge in Illyria. Thence they crossed into Upper Macedonia, and went to the town of Lebaea, where they hired themselves to do menial work for the king ... even the reigning houses were of slender means, and in Lebaea the king's wife cooked the food. Now it happened that every time she baked, the loaf intended for the boy Perdiccas swelled to double its size. She said nothing for a time, but when it went on happening every time, she told her husband. At once it occurred to the king that it was a warning from heaven of some important event, so he sent for the three brothers, and ordered them to leave the country. They ... said they had a right to their wages, and would go as soon as they had been paid. The sun was shining through a smoke hole in the roof, and the king ... cried out 'I give you the wages you deserve – there they are!' and pointed to the sun. The two elder brothers were struck dumb, but the boy – Perdiccas – who had a knife, scratched a line with the point of it round the patch of sunlight on the floor, and said 'King, we accept what you offer us.' Then, three times he made as if to collect the sunlight into the folds of his tunic, and left the town with his brothers. When they had gone someone in attendance on the king mentioned what a significant thing the boy had done. The king was angry, and ordered men to ride in pursuit of the brothers, and kill them. In this part of the country there is a river to which the descendants of these three men offer sacrifice as their saviour – for when they crossed it, it suddenly rose so high that their pursuers were unable to

1 View from Edessa towards Mt. Vermion

get over. Once safe on the other side the brothers went on to another part of Macedonia, and settled near a place called the Garden of Midas – a place where wonderful roses grew wild ... blooms with sixty petals, and sweeter smelling than any others ... Above them rises Mount Bermion [Vermion] the heights of which are so cold that none can climb them, and it was from the slopes of these mountains that the brothers conquered first the land in the immediate neighbourhood, and afterwards the whole of Macedonia.

Mount Vermion rises to more than 6,000 feet, and to this day there is a village called Perdikka, north of Kozani, and near Lake Cheikaditis.

Thucydides (2.99) gives a lucid account, and also deals in some detail with the son of Perdiccas II, King Archelaos, whose dating was 413–399 BC, and who was one of the greatest of the Macedonian kings – probably second only to Philip II. Perdiccas II (450–413 BC) by alliances and diplomacy, as well as by war, succeeded in uniting Macedonia, and this enabled Archelaos to consolidate the position in the country, create a competent military organisation and also to build good roads, particularly on the northern plain. Archelaos' cavalry had magnificent horses, which were superior to those used by the Thracians in battle. He also created a following in Larissa, south of Mount Olympos. Among other forward-looking developments, he moved the court from Aegae to Pella, although the former remained the cult-centre, and the place of royal burial was still near Vergina.

Pella was at that time on a deep inlet from the Thermaic gulf, reached from the sea by the mouths of two rivers, and a lake, which has since silted up. At the head of this lake was a little town named Bounomos, and it was here that the king realised would be an excellent site for the capital city of Macedon. Because of the lake, it was possible to build a harbour, and there was good protection from the east and therefore from Thrace by the river Axios. Archelaos changed the name of the town from Bounomos to Pella, and set up a court of some magnificence, to which he invited distinguished citizens of Athens – such as the great tragic poets Euripides and Agathon – and the historian Thucydides appears to write of it from personal knowledge. A short stanza, ascribed to him, commemorates the death of Euripides, which took place after the poet had voluntarily exiled himself to Macedon, but it does not appear to prove that Thucydides was at Archelaos' court, although he may have been.

> 'Greece is thy monument, Euripides,
> In Macedon laid, where thou didst end thy days,
> Thy country Athens, veriest Greece of Greece,
> The Muse thy joy, and everywhere thy praise.

Hippocrates also came and settled at the Macedonian court, and during this time spent three years on the island of Thasos.

Later, much of the strength of Macedonia which Archelaos created during his reign was dissipated, partly because of troubles of succession after his death, and partly through the over-running of the country by the Illyrians shortly after the accession of Amyntas (393–370 BC). There followed a period of trouble and unrest, with the country changing hands, and with interference from the Chalkidian League, until Amyntas entered into an alliance with Athens in 373 BC. This was followed by a period of some economic growth and progress.

His eldest son, Alexander, created a force known as the 'Foot Companions'. According to Herodotus (8.137) '... this Alexander was descended in the seventh generation from Perdiccas, who won the lordship of Macedonia ...' After only one year as king, Alexander was assassinated by Ptolemy, who reigned from 368–365, when he was displaced by Amyntas' eldest surviving son – again called Perdiccas.

There followed a period of varying fortune, during which the coastal cities of Methone and Pydna were lost, and the king was also compelled to enter into a treaty with Amphipolis, as well as with the Chalkidian League.

In 362 BC, Perdiccas, who had for some time endeavoured to capture Amphipolis, decided to change his allegiance, and sent part of his army to fight for Amphipolis against Athens. Seven years later he attacked on his western frontier, but was killed by the Illyrians, as were 4,000 of his men.

After this shattering defeat, it was essential for the Macedonians to create some sort of stability in their country. Perdiccas' son, Amyntas, was only an infant, and the state elected his uncle, Philip – a younger brother of Perdiccas – as Regent.

Philip had been taken prisoner, and had been held as a hostage in Thebes from 367–364 BC, and had made good use of his time, learning not only the arts of war, but also the greater skills of diplomacy.

Diplomacy – often a loosely-used term – means, not only 'the art of international relations by negotiation' but also 'skill in intercourse of any kind'. The future was to show that Philip was indeed a master of this skill, and had learned much from his association in Thebes with Epaminondas, and from the strategy which ended Sparta's supremacy in Greece.

It is sad for posterity that Herodotus died before Philip was born, so we are left without the vivid description of this Macedonian king which the great historian would undoubtedly have given us.

Philip was twenty-two years old when his brother died, and his immediate policy was to divide his enemies. Two of his brothers, as well as many other Macedonians, were disloyal to him, and one of these – a pretender to the throne called Pausanias – was backed by Berisades, the king of Thrace. Philip won over, some say bought off, Berisades who at once murdered Pausanias. Two of Philip's brothers, who were in fact half-brothers, sought the protection of the Chalkidian League, and the third was assassinated.

Philip then withdrew the Macedonian troops from Amphipolis and attacked and won a great victory against Paeonia in 358 BC.

He next fought a superbly planned battle against the king of Illyria, Bardylis, with the result that Bardylis ceded much territory to him; and also gave him an Illyrian princess in marriage. Philip's victory against Illyria withdrew some of the immense pressure which this state had hitherto exerted against Epirus, to the south-west – occupied by the Molossian peoples; in consequence their king, Neoptolemus (Pyrros) gave his daughter Olympias to Philip, not only in marriage but as his queen. Shortly before this, the Macedonians had deposed Philip's nephew Amyntas, and elected Philip as King Philip II of Macedon. Olympias remained his queen throughout his life, although in all he had six wives. Thus came about the union of the two royal houses of Epirus and Macedonia, two states with not only one boundary in common, but many other similarities; to the subsequent benefit of both. Epirus, at Dodona, had an Oracle of Zeus, and it was to this Oracle that *theoroi* were sent from Macedonia more frequently than to the Oracle at Delphi. Many Macedonians also travelled to Dodona in person to ask their questions, and as we shall see in a later chapter, many and varied were these questions and their replies.

Later, in the days of Antigonos Gonotas, the Molossian king requested help from Macedonia, in the shape of men and of money, both of which Antigonos gave him. Later he changed sides in the fashion not unusual in northern Greece, and took possession of Upper Macedonia.

The Molossian (Epirus) arms were always dedicated to Athena Itonia – a sanctuary not yet found – but '... to Zeus, at Dodona, he (Pyrros) dedicated the round shields of the Macedonians themselves ...' (Pausanias 1.13), and the dedication was engraved thereon.

> This metal destroyed Asia rich in gold
> this metal made slaves out of the Greeks
> this metal is lying fatherless
> by the pillars of Zeus of water-streams   [Dodona]
> the spoil of proud-voiced Macedonia.'

There can be no question that Philip II created the true greatness of Macedonia, and was responsible for bringing almost supreme power in Greece to the state, although solid foundations had been laid originally by Archelaos. Philip unified the east and the west and gave protection to the island of Thasos at the same time taking over the Thasian gold-mines at Mount Pangaean. He also changed the name of their colony there from Krenides to Philippi. He

recaptured the ports of Pydna and Methone, and united Thrace, Thessaly and Chalkidiki with a common coinage from the royal Macedonian mint, thus creating sufficient economic strength to maintain a permanent and well-equipped army. He made peace with Athens in 346 BC, and ended the war which had lasted so long.

Philip's great cause, and life's work, was the state or kingdom of Macedonia, and to its creation and consolidation he contributed brilliantly and lastingly. Modern scholastic thought is divided about his personality, but no one questions his great statesmanship, and brilliant achievements.

Isocrates recognised in almost prophetic fashion that the way of salvation for Greece was neither through Sparta nor Athens, but that it was through Macedonia and through Philip that it would come. In 346 BC he wrote '... you alone have the great authority given you by Destiny, to send ambassadors to whom you will, to receive them from whom you think fit, to say what you think advantageous; you are in possession moreover of power such as no Greek has ever had; the only things there are that can both persuade – and compel ...' (Isocrates, *Philip*, 14.15)

Above everything Philip possessed the gift of leadership, and this produced results in Macedonia which are obvious to this day. Anywhere and at any time that a real leader is giving to his country the benefits of his vision, his wisdom and the overwhelming belief he must have in the rightness of his cause, the results will last for posterity.

It is impossible to condense into a few sentences the results of the ability and the organisation of this man, let alone his conquests. In Professor N. G. H. Hammond's *History of Greece to 322 BC*, he devotes two long chapters to Philip II's achievements, which make exhilarating reading, but as the object of this book is to explore the great archaeological sites which are left to us and enable us to verify many of the facts of his life, only a brief outline can be given here.

In 336 BC Cleopatra – the sister of Alexander the Great and daughter of Philip and his queen Olympias – was marrying her uncle, Alexander I, king of Molossia, thereby further uniting the kingdoms of Molossia (Epirus) and Macedonia. During the celebrations Philip was entering the theatre at Aegae when he was assassinated by a young nobleman named Pausanias. Philip, who was forty-six years old, had for once been unaccompanied by the royal guards. It was a tragic, almost unbearable ending for one of the most brilliant men that the world has ever seen.

When he was killed he was not only king of Macedon but *archon* of the Thessalian League, ruler over the heads of his vassal states, a financial delegate to the Amphictyonic Council and *hegemon* to the Greek League in time of war.

It would appear, as is underlined by Professor Hammond, that Philip was a deeply religious man, and that his ability was much assisted by the integrity that is thus created.

In all things Philip was truly Greek, except – as one critic comments – he drank more than is normal with the Greeks. He claimed descent from Zeus through Herakles, and from that Alexander who had proved his Argive descent before the Council of the Olympic Games, and had competed in a foot race, in which he had tied equal first. (Herodotos 5. 23)

The heads of Zeus, Apollo and Herakles were on his coins.

His eldest son, later to be known as Alexander the Great, inherited a stable kingdom, possessed of great power in Greece, and he was therefore able to put into action his father's plan for the invasion of Persia, which Philip had been about to undertake when he was assassinated. Much thought and trouble had gone into Alexander's preparation and education for kingship. Philip had employed Aristotle, who was a Macedonian born at Stagiros in the Chalkidiki, as his tutor and he had grown up at the court at Pella in an atmosphere of almost Athenian civilisation. So much has been written of Alexander, his brilliant campaigns, and his ambition for deification, that only brief mention will be made of him here. However, it is unlikely that his conquests of so many countries could have taken place without the creation and consolidation by his father of the state of Macedonia. Nonetheless Alexander was passionately Macedonian despite his almost continuous absence from his country.

Macedonia – a brief background

During the fourth century BC there were public sacrifices in Athens to Zeus-Ammon, whose original cult was at the Siwa Oasis in Egypt. This cult was, of course, Egypto-Greek, as Ammon or Amun, also in Egypt Amun-Re, was the all-powerful god of the Egyptian pantheon, whom the Greeks equated with their own great god, Zeus. In the later part of his life it was to Zeus-Ammon that Alexander mainly sacrificed, although he must have sacrificed to Herakles – the hero-ancestor of the Argaedae – and to other Greek gods as well.

His life was played on too large a stage to confine himself to his small state, and with this, towards the end of his life, went a belief that his inspiration was semi-divine, and that he was a son of Zeus.

After Alexander the kingship of Macedonia passed to the Antigonid family of whom probably the most noteworthy was Antigonas II, surnamed Gonatas. He succeeded Demetrios and, having lost much of Thessaly to Pyrrhus, took the title of king of Macedon in 283 BC. His achievements are dealt with in some detail in the chapter on Aegae, the ancient capital of Macedonia before its move to Pella by King Archelaos; and his tomb is almost certainly in the great tumulus there which contains the royal burials.

Antigonas Gonatas was succeeded by Antigonas III, who had been the guardian of Philip, later V of Macedon. He assumed the kingship in 227 BC shortly after marrying Philip's widowed mother, Phthia. Philip became king in 221 BC. His military ability was, apparently, very considerable, but his achievements were hampered by his unstable personality.

Chapter 2

Aegae – the ancient capital

The first known capital of Macedonia was the city of Aegae, from which King Archelaos (413–399 BC) moved his court to Pella, although Aegae remained the royal cult-centre. The exact position of the original capital is still uncertain, although recent excavation is beginning to show some light through the mists of uncertainty. Unfortunately there is no help from Herodotus who makes no mention of the Macedonian city, only briefly mentioning Aegae in Achaea.

For a considerable time the excavations at Edessa, in the north-west, caused archaeologists to believe that this site was the ancient capital. It had also been called Vodena, and was in a strong position between the Macedonian plain and north-western Macedonia and Illyria. However the recent magnificent discoveries at Vergina near the great burial site and palace there have cast doubts on this belief, and scholastic opinion is coming round to the fact that Vergina is, in fact, ancient Aegae.

The site at Vergina is surely more likely to have been the capital, from the extent and magnificence of its position and remains, and it is possible that Edessa, which is near, but not on, the slopes of Mount Vermion, could be the Lebaea of Herodotus in Book 8.137. Perdiccas and his brothers, as we have seen in chapter 1, settled 'near' a place called the Garden of Midas, and Professor Nicholas Hammond, well-known as an authority on northern Greece, claims that Edessa was 'the' Garden of Midas. The distance to the slopes of Mount Vermion is not very great, and a river would have to be crossed to get there from Edessa.

The archaeological site there is in a beautiful position surrounded by vineyards and fruit orchards. It is below the little modern town, which stands high on a hill, with immense waterfalls rushing to the valley below. It is a place with a great atmosphere of peace broken only by the sound of innumerable cicadas, and the occasional voice of a labourer on the 'dig'; and in the spring there is the song of large numbers of nightingales. Above, in the distance, are the waterfalls which are the great feature of modern Edessa, and there is a mule-track from the hills which just avoids the edge of stratographic digging on the ancient site.

The main excavations form a large oblong, orientated just east-of-north and west-of-south, with a straight main street paved with marble. The gate, which is wide enough to enable chariots to pass through, is at the southern end, and the hooks for the hinges and the opening mechanism are plain to see. The walls at the southern end are immensely thick, of good ashlar masonry, although the wall to the west of the gate, which is based on natural rock, is cut or damaged. An interesting feature is the extensive piped water supply.

On each side of the main street there are standing Ionic columns, and one Corinthian column – with its capital – has been excavated, but has not yet been re-erected. From the modern town above there is a lovely, almost aerial view of the site as a whole. Unfortunately the museum in Edessa is frequently closed, so it is difficult to view the finds from the excavations which are kept there, but the tombs on the site are of some interest, and a number of coins – among other things – have been found.

Some fifty-five kilometres south of Edessa is the village of Vergina, the archaeological site of which was originally excavated by a Frenchman called Leon Heuzey in 1861. Here is the contestant with Edessa for the site of the city of Aegae, and today there are not many people who will argue against Vergina's being the ancient capital.

Few people can today be unaware of the tremendous discovery in October 1977 of two royal tombs, one of which was un-plundered. The archaeologist responsible for this find, with his team, was Professor Manolis Andronicos, of the University of Thessaloniki, and the unplundered tomb contained large quantities

2 Piped water supply. Edessa

of gold, silver and bronze artifacts, jewellery, and much else, which included cremated remains. These will be discussed later in this chapter in some detail.

The original excavation of Leon Heuzey was carried on only after a considerable interval, mainly caused by Turkish occupation of Macedonia, and various political and national changes of fortune for northern Greece. In 1937 a Greek professor, K. A. Rhomaios, continued the work which had been begun earlier, and from 1954 until 1959 – again after an interval of time – was joined by the Curator of Antiquities for Macedonia, an archaeologist called Makaronas. From 1959 onwards two Greek professors of Classical archaeology – Balalakis and Andronicos – have directed the excavations at Vergina.

A short distance from the village there is a very large area of tumuli, known as the Cemetery of Mounds – a necropolis dating to 1000 BC. These mounds vary from 5 to 20 metres in circumference, and are from 2 to 3 metres high. Almost in the village was one colossal tumulus, covering a width of 100 metres, and it is in this tumulus that the royal tombs have been found.

The small mounds in the main necropolis have yielded many finds of interest and value, including vases, weapons and jewellery; and, as always, the pottery has enabled accurate dating to be recorded.

The mounds contained varying numbers of burials, but the archaeologists concluded that each mound belonged to one family. The most important finds were from female burials as the women were always buried wearing their best clothes, and all the jewellery that they possessed. They were mainly clad in the *peplos*, held on the shoulder by a brooch.

Amphorae were buried with the dead, generally two in number, to hold wine and oil or water, and there would also have been some form of food. Later than the pre-historic period, the contents of the tombs were not, archaeologically, of significant value until the great find of the royal tombs in 1977.

That year, and with considerable difficulty, two royal tombs were discovered. Both tombs were built, with slabs of stone to

3 Entrance and main road. Site at Edessa

protect the doors, and vast mural paintings on the outside above these doors; and the first found had been completely looted. However it contained a very fine wall-painting, which is thought may be attributable to the Macedonian painter, Nikomachos, portraying the Rape of Persephone (Kore), the daughter of Demeter, the corn goddess. It has been said that Kore is being raped by Pluto, but this surely should be a matter for further discussion. Pluto is the Latin name for Hades – a son of Kronos, and brother of the great god, Zeus. He is once mentioned in the *Iliad*, as Zeus Katachthonios (beneath the earth), and as Persephone's husband. However, two of the best-known scholars of Greek mythology, Farnell and Nilsson, hold that Persephone was originally the consort not of Hades, but of Plouton – the god of the great wealth produced by the earth, particularly corn – who is also mentioned by Hesiod in the *Theogony*. Demeter is shown in this wall-painting seated beside a chariot, which is of particular interest because the axle is made of wood.

The second royal tomb has a magnificent and very well-preserved painting of a lion hunt on its façade, and contained treasure which has not been surpassed in Greece since the finds of Heinrich Schliemann at Mycenae, just a hundred years before. The mural, which is of great interest since it shows that these vast paintings were also done in Macedonia, and not only in the more sophisticated south, was created by an artist who knew something of the art of perspective. It is very well preserved, and shows horsemen as well as hunters on foot, searching for a lion in a huge forest of trees.

Entry to this tomb had to be made through a small opening which the archaeologists were able to pierce in the roof. Within were two rooms, both richly furnished and quite untouched. Each room contained a decorated, gold-sheathed box inside a marble container, and the lids were decorated with the radiating star of Macedonia. Cremated remains were within, each wrapped in a cloth, which was embroidered in silver and gold. The cremated remains were bones and ashes; the fact that there were bones is significant, in that the cremation had been – as was usual at this

4 Site of Royal Tombs at Vergina

time – on a funeral pyre. The tomb also contained outstanding funerary offerings which included vases of gold, silver and bronze; and weapons and armour picked out in gold. The burials are attributed by the archaeologists to 330–340 BC.

A most interesting fact is that oak leaves and branches covered the cremated remains, and there was a gold filigree semi-circular jewel of exquisite workmanship of acorns and oakleaves also. This would suggest that the owner of the tomb was a follower of the Cult of Zeus at Dodona, which was the oldest known Oracle in Greece, and would also suggest that he had some association with the royal house of Epirus, the Molossi. The cult of Zeus and his earliest consort, Dione, known as 'the Earth Mother', is known to have been practised at Dodona as early as the fourteenth-thirteenth centuries BC, and it was still fashionable for the Macedonian people to consult the Oracle there as late as the fourth-third century BC. Silver coins, which were minted in the third century BC, show Zeus and Dione with a bull, surrounded by a wreath of oak leaves.

It is known that when King Archelaos moved the court from Aegae to Pella the former remained the cult-centre; and it is therefore obvious that it also remained the place of royal burial; and since the discovery of these tombs there seems little doubt that Vergina is, indeed, Aegae. There is also much evidence for the unplundered tomb being that of Philip of Macedon. Discovery of a theatre in this area would be very considerable additional proof.

Professor Andronicos and his team had excavated for forty-one days in 1977 with no result except the recovery of a large number of broken gravestones, and remains of destroyed tombs, and were digging a new trench for the next season of excavations when the workmen came upon two walls, and the sides of the two built tombs. These have given to the world some of the most magnificent treasure which has been discovered in Greece, or elsewhere.

In August 1978, only a few days before the author of this book visited the Professor on site at Vergina, another built tomb was found, and this again had not been broken into by thieves. From the contents this appeared also to have been a royal burial, but the tomb had been hastily sealed, presumably owing to the humidity

5 Macedonian tomb near the palace at Vergina. Façade built to represent an Ionian temple, with a frieze of painted flowers

of the climate, and everything had apparently been completed with very great haste. The cremated remains within were only partially burnt, and some of the oakleaves and acorns had been dropped outside. The tomb was built in much the same manner as the second (unplundered) one, with a central door covered with stone blocks, and a vast mural painting on the façade; however this third tomb contained a magnificently designed and painted frieze of chariots on the inside – high on the walls. The colour, design and perspective of this frieze is outstanding, and no two chariots are alike. They are painted in shades of terra cotta and deep peacock blue as the main colours, and are obviously being driven very fast. Their state of preservation is remarkable. This tomb was also filled with gold, silver and bronze objects, but it is yet too early (December 1978) for much cleaning and preservation work to have been done. However, one small ivory has been photographed and shown, of the god Dionysos, with Ariadne, and a third figure who is thought to be Pan.

Some of the finds from Vergina are already on view in the museum at Thessaloniki, and will be described in Chapter 9.

On the south-eastern side of the village is another built tomb – with a façade like a small temple. This tomb was excavated in 1937–38 by Professor Rhomios, who was, among others, assisted by a second-year student from the University of Thessaloniki called Manolis Andronicos.

The façade of this tomb is that of a small Ionian temple, with four half-columns, and a decorated frieze of painted flowers. The outer door, which now lies on the floor of the ante-chamber of the tomb, is unusual, being constructed of marble which is carved to look like studded wood. Within, at the graveside, is the usual table for offerings for the funerary feast; or a vase containing the ashes could have stood on it. A marble throne which is damaged stands in the right-hand corner of the inner chamber with winged sphinxes supporting each arm, and carvings of gryphons attacking a deer – a subject often seen in Macedonia – painted on the side. This tomb is of the Hellenistic period (323–27 BC) and had been completely robbed before it was discovered by the archaeologists.

Above this, on a hill, in a very fine position with beautiful views, are the considerable remains of an Hellenistic palace, now thought to have been built on the site of an earlier construction. This Hellenistic structure is likely to have been built by Antigonos Gonatos, who reigned from 276–239 BC; he had marched on Macedonia, but was repulsed, although later – with help – he won a victory over the state, and also won over the allegiance of its people. Like Archelaos before him he gathered men of intelligence and culture round him, and his court contained many poets, philosophers and historians; and he re-established Macedonia as a nation – something which had been sadly lacking after Philip II's assassination, and Alexander the Great's almost permanent absence overseas.

The palace is over 100 metres long, and 80 metres wide, with one fine mosaic still extant in room 13, to which there is a marble threshold. Unhappily many other mosaics have been destroyed, and it is thought that their destruction was not accidental, but because erotic scenes, and depictions of the old gods, were not acceptable to later, Christian occupation.

Most of the building is of the local *poros*, a stone which is common throughout Greece, although some marble has been incorporated in the thresholds. From the northern side there is a very fine view of the valley of the Aliakmon river.

No theatre has, as yet, been excavated for this city, and its discovery is much needed, as it would go far to give absolute confirmation that this was the place where Philip II of Macedon was murdered.

His son and successor, Alexander the Great, is said to have expressed a wish not to be buried in the royal necropolis at Aegae, but in the Temple of Zeus Ammon – whose descendant he claimed to be – in the Siwa Oasis in Egypt, or possibly at that god's temple in Athens. This cannot have pleased the Macedonian people, many of whom had not approved of his government of the country, and his continuous journeyings.

The Cemetery of Mounds dates, as we have seen, from the Iron Age, 1000 BC, and the urgent requirement now would seem to be the discovery of at least foundations earlier than the Hellenistic period, near the site of the palace.

Chapter 3

Pella

When Archelaos, king of Macedonia (413–399 BC) decided that it would be advantageous to move the court and the administration from Aegae, he chose a site on an inlet from the Thermaic Gulf. Beyond the gulf, inland, was a deep lake which is now silted up, and near this lake was a little town named Bounomos. Here was undoubtedly a most suitable place to build his new capital city; accessible to both eastern and western Macedonia, and with the necessary access to the sea for a harbour to be established.

Archelaos was an enlightened king who had built straight roads and bridged the rivers, and had also strengthened the fortifications throughout Macedonia, and when he moved his court he decided that it should become as brilliant and as intellectual as anything in Greece. He changed the name of the little town from Bounomos to Pella, and built fine buildings, paved with pebble mosaics, which archaeological excavation has brought to light since 1957.

There had been a brief excavation in 1914 – immediately after Macedonia was liberated from Turkey, and although these excavations were brought to an end almost at once by the onset of the 1914–18 war, the archaeologist – Oikonomos – had discovered some fine bronzes, and part of a house. Sometime earlier a fifth century BC gravestone representing a young soldier had been found, proving some form of occupation of the Archaic period. Although the court had been moved to Pella, the royal cult-centre is said to have remained at Aegae, and certainly the necropolis is still there.

Pella was known to Herodotus, and from him we have proof that it was on the sea, as he refers to '. . . a small strip of coastline occupied by . . . and Pella . . .' and it became not only the capital, but the largest city of Macedonia until overtaken in importance by Thessaloniki in AD 146.

Pella

Having established his capital city, with its harbour, Archelaos decided that he would invite philosophers, poets and scholars to join him there, and in a short time he had attracted a brilliant following which included the tragedian Agathon; the lyric poet Timotheus; and above all one of the great tragic poets of all time – Euripides – who left Athens for Pella in 408 BC, and died there, or nearby, in 406 BC. It has been said that the King invited Socrates, who refused on the grounds that life at the Macedonian court would be too expensive for him.

Euripides wrote three plays whilst he was at Pella – the *Archelaos*, which was lost, and must have been about the king; the *Iphigeneia in Aulis* and the *Bacchae*, both of which, to the great benefit of scholarship, have survived. The *Iphigeneia* is a most unusual play, with a different type of dynamic action from those that the poet had hitherto written; and its opening scene also differs from the normal form of prologue. The *Bacchae*, which few will deny was his greatest play, is unique in that it is the only known play to present a contemporary picture of a great religion which was being followed throughout Greece during Euripides' lifetime. There is little question that the Macedonian influence of the court at Pella had a considerable effect on the great playwright. It is said that Euripides was a follower of the Sophists – those 'sophisticated' Greeks who claimed that all knowledge and all decision was centred in man, and not in god. If this was so, then Euripides' thinking underwent a considerable change when he wrote this play; a change which would help to explain the underlying passionate struggle which haunts so much of the poet's work. Always there is a feeling of tension, and of a deep desire for a truth which appears to elude him, and there are, consequently, swift contradictions of outlook and mood in his later work which are so particularly noticeable in the *Bacchae*. In the *Suppliant Women*, written much earlier, we have a strangely calm acceptance of life, from the lips of Theseus:

> ... I believe
> that there are more good things than bad for mortals
> If there were not, the light would not be ours.

Pella

> I praise the god who set our life in order
> Lifting it out of savagery and confusion.
> First he put wits in us, then gave language
> Envoy of words – to understand the voice;
> And fruits of earth to eat ...

but at other times the passion and unhappiness created by Euripides is almost unbearable. It is obvious that it is human existence, with its tragic implications, that is his real concern, and in places he deliberately alters the traditional myths to suit this purpose. There is an obvious instance of this in the *Herakles*. The god is supposed, in the myth, to have killed his wife and children in a fit of madness, as the *result* of which he had to serve Eurystheus; and the Labours followed. However, in the play Euripides clearly wishes to underline once again the extent of good and evil in man – the distance between the heights which can be reached by him (in Herakles' case in the Labours, and his *subsequent* warm welcome to his children) which are followed by the depths of his humiliation. In Herakles' case the ultimate humiliation was his own suicide, preceded by utter despair, which leads him to say 'O god is hard, and I hard against god ...'

As always, Professor Albin Lesky has summed up the poet's work with great understanding when he says that the Chorus of old men in the *Herakles* sing of his life's task.

> Never shall I cease from this –
> Muses with the Graces joining,
> loveliness in yoke together.
> I may not live without the Muses.
> Let my head be always crowned!
> May my old age always sing
> of Memory, the Muses' mother,
> always shall I sing the crown
> of Herakles the victor!
> So long as these remain –
> Dionysos' gift of wine,

6 The great court at Pella – to which King Archelaos moved the
Macedonian court, from Aegae

Pella

the lyre of seven strings
the shrilling of the flute –
never shall I cease to sing
Muses who made me dance!'

The two plays which were written at Pella bring out more strongly than any of the others the great inner conflict in Euripides, but they are undoubtedly the triumph of all his writing. In the *Bacchae* there is the first-hand account of the god Dionysos, who at that time dominated the worship of the Macedonians, as well as a large part of the rest of Greece, and in whose cult tragedy had originated; and in the *Iphigeneia* it is surely difficult not to see the poet's comments on himself in some words of Agamemnon in the opening scene:

'I envy you, old man. I envy any man that has lived a life of quiet days, unknown to fame ... glory is perilous; honour is sweet, but it is also the near neighbour of grief.'

In addition to attracting a brilliant following to his court, Archelaos also celebrated Games at Dium, and introduced Persian coinage to Macedonia, which considerably helped the economy. Some fifty years later, in 336 BC, a son was born at Pella to Olympias, wife of Philip II. He was later to be known as Alexander the Great, and in the Pella museum there is an Hellenistic head of him typical of the impression which is given by artists of this period, rather girlish in feature.

The excavations to date cover a large area, and are a good example of later Classical and early Hellenistic building. The most impressive is a great court with Ionic columns which, with so many standing, makes the approach to this site very lovely. A piped water-supply everywhere is evident, and among important finds were numbers of roof-tiles, stamped with the single word Pella. The lettering was of the late fourth century BC, and beautifully engraved. Other tiles were found, marked with proper names, and also with the word *basilikos*, which at this period means a royal building, and not, as it did later, a great church.

7 Pebble mosaic at Pella, from which Dionysos riding on his panther was removed, and is now in the museum there

Pella

There is a small museum opposite the gates of the main site which is well-designed, and unlike so many museums the light inside is excellent. Among a number of interesting objects on display is a large marble measure used for liquids, presumably oil and wine, and the kraters are bell-shaped, but without handles. There are a number of bronzes and terra cottas, and the usual small lamps and votive vases. A rather beautiful bas-relief marble, which could be a funerary stele, shows a seated figure, possibly of a god, holding the hand of a woman, and there is a child beneath.

Amongst the red-figure pottery is a fine *pelike* of the fourth century BC, and there is a late Hellenistic bronze figure of the god Poseidon, said to be a copy of Lysippean work. Lysippos worked for some years in Macedonia, and found much favour with Alexander the Great. A funerary figure of a dog, which is beautifully modelled, found on a tomb at Pella, is thought by some to be of the Archaic period, but Professor Andronicos is of the opinion that it is early Classical, which would seem to be more likely. A small terra cotta statuette of the goddess Athena, though late, is of much interest, as she is wearing a helmet with horns, which appear to be those of a cow. Cow's horns are an attribute of a number of ancient cults, and were worn, for instance, by the Egyptian goddess Hathor. This statuette is, almost certainly, a copy of the cult-statue of Athena which stood in her temple at Pella, where she was worshipped as Athena Alkidemos.

Athena, who was one of the Olympian Twelve, was – according to Hesiod – 'grey-eyed', from whom 'comes all the race of womenkind, the deadly female race, and tribe of wives …' She was born, full-grown, from the head of Zeus, and was worshipped throughout Greece in many forms. She was always regarded as virgin, as a war-goddess, as a patron of crafts such as spinning and weaving, as Poliouchos – protectress of the city – and in many more guises. Scholars have proved, more or less conclusively, that she was a pre-Hellenic goddess, but at the time of Pella, according to Professor Rose, her importance from Sparta to Macedonia was second only to that of Zeus himself. In her Homeric hymn she is described as a 'renowned goddess, dark-eyed, of much counsel; possessing an

8 Stag mosaic at Pella

un-softened heart; a hallowed virgin, guardian of cities, valiant . . .' but elsewhere, as in Hesiod, she is always described as grey-eyed.

Unfortunately, with the coming of the Romans, there was much plundering in Pella, and many of the more valuable possessions of the Macedonians were stolen; however, underneath a very shallow soil layer, archaeologists found pebble mosaics which surpass those discovered at Olynthos.

Some of these mosaics have been removed to the museum for safety from climatic changes, but others are undergoing cleaning and restoration on site. In the museum is a magnificent mosaic of Dionysos, riding on his panther. The god is sitting sideways, in an elegant, easy fashion, although the impression of the whole figure is rather feminine. It would appear, from the many representations of Dionysos, that in the late Classical and Hellenistic periods the Greek artists and sculptors tended to interpret his features and form in a slightly girlish manner. Although there is little colour in this mosaic, except for the wreath of vineleaves on his head, and the be-ribboned *thyrsos* he holds in his left hand, the whole effect is extremely beautiful. This, as were most of the others, is a floor mosaic. In the building in which this was found there was another mosaic, representing a lion-hunt, and here the figures are far more virile, and decidedly more male. The perspective in this composition is impressive for the period, and there is a considerable feeling of movement, not only in the lion's head, and lashing tail, but also in the two hunters – one of whom holds a short sword, and the other a spear; and one of them is wearing the well-known Macedonian hat, which is known as a *kausia*.

Two more floor mosaics were found in a second building – one, which unhappily is clumsy and with no great beauty of design or execution, represents Amazons. The other is not only a work of real merit, but it is signed by the oldest named mosaicist – Gnosis. This very fine composition represents two men killing a stag, assisted by a dog. The perspective is excellent, and again there is a real feeling of movement, particularly with the men's cloaks, which are blowing in the wind. The main scene is surrounded by a frieze of tendrils and flowers, in a very delicate design, and above is the inscription 'Gnosis made this'. The dating of this and the other mosaics is approximately 300 BC, and in all cases the tesserae are pebbles.

Outside, beside the standing Ionic columns, is a good example of a geometric pattern mosaic floor, in black and white, and there are more which have been recently excavated depicting a variety of subjects.

Work at Pella continues every season, and some interesting recent discoveries have been made, but so far all tests have failed to locate the theatre. However, part of the city's fortified wall has been brought to light, and there has also been work on the sophisticated water and drainage systems.

Pella was built in a magnificent position, and before the coast receded approach by sea must have been truly impressive. Today, driving west from Thessaloniki, Pella is still a lovely sight, and the excellent modern museum is an added attraction for this ancient Macedonian capital.

Pella was, of course, the site of the court of Philip II and his queen, Olympias, and there are many historical references to the city during his reign. The city by the time of Philip's accession had a thriving port, and during his reign the harbour dues were sold for some forty talents. Later his capture of both Pydna and Methone on the western Macedonian coast removed threats from the sea, and by 353 BC he controlled the entire coast from Mount Olympos in the south to the river Nestos on the borders of Thrace in eastern Macedonia.

The coins minted at Pella had a wide circulation, and among emblems on them of the god, Herakles, and also of Philip himself, was one of a boy rider on a horse of the king's which had won at the Olympic Games.

It was at Pella, in 346 BC, that Philip received the envoys from Athens, suing for peace with Macedonia, and it was to Pella that Philip summoned Aristotle, in 342 BC, to become tutor to his son Alexander.

Chapter 4

Olynthos – Amphipolis

Olynthos became a Greek city in 479 BC, after its previous capture by the Persians, and it is the most important Archaic site remaining on the three-pronged promontory of the Chalkidiki.

As early as 600 BC the Corinthians had founded a colony named Potidaea, on the western side of the Chalkidiki, to enable them to carry on their trade with Macedonia more easily than was possible from their native land, south of the Gulf of Corinth; and later, the city of Olynthos was built immediately to the north of Potidaea. Its position, between two of the three peninsulas of the Chalkidiki, and near, but not on, the sea, made it a natural centre for the local Greeks to defend themselves from attacks from Athens and Sparta, and also from Macedonia. Later, according to the historian Thucydides (1.58) the then king of Macedonia, Perdiccas, persuaded the Chalkidian Greeks to abandon their coastal cities, such as Potidaea, and all to settle in Olynthos, thereby making it one big city and easier to defend. To help persuade the Olynthians he offered them land from Mygdonia as additional protection, at any rate as long as the war with Athens continued. The city prospered, and soon became the centre of a Chalkidian League, issuing its own coinage, which is always a sign of growing prosperity.

There is little really accurate evidence for events which took place later, and there has been much argument about their sequence, particularly from 351 BC to 349 BC, but it does appear that after Philip II became king of Macedonia the Olynthians tried to negotiate a separate alliance with Athens while constantly assuring Philip that they would do nothing without him. With his usual diplomacy Philip warned them not to 'encourage War and Violence' within their city, but at the same time he strengthened the Macedonian party who were already living there; and on one occasion, returning from an expedition to Thrace, he marched through Olynthian territory accompanied by his army. The march was entirely peaceful, and without incident, and was doubtless merely a show of strength. Eventually an alliance between Macedonia and Olynthos was made, which was essential to Philip if he was to subdue the Macedonian ports both to the west and to the east. This is shown plainly by the map, since unless the king could count on Olynthian loyalty he could be stabbed in the back while attacking either way.

Unfortunately, Demosthenes – who is referred to as the greatest of the Athenian orators – was a bitter opponent of the king, and, in a series of brilliant orations known as *Philippics*, and also as *Olynthics*, accused him of perfidy and treachery; and he also attacked the motive for most of the things which the king was doing or trying to do. In two Olynthic orations he spoke of the Thessalians becoming restless under Philip's supremacy, and their objection to his appropriation of their market and harbour dues, without, in any way, referring to the benefits Thessaly had obtained from Philip's protection. In all, Demosthenes delivered four *Philippics*, but many of his other orations inveighed against the king of Macedonia. Philip, without doubt, aroused violent, and violently opposed, feelings among a large number of people. Here we have two great Athenians, Isocrates and Demosthenes, whose lives overlapped for nearly fifty years, with passionately different views of the king. Both were Athenian; both were alive during almost the whole of his reign. Isocrates – the elder – lived from 436–338 BC, Demosthenes, who was not born until 384 BC died in 322 BC. Of the two, Isocrates was the lesser orator, lacking the overbearing self-confidence of Demosthenes. Both, however, through their oratory, ceaselessly gave the king advice.

In the winter of 357 BC, despite persistent advances from Athens to Olynthos, a defensive alliance between Macedonia and the Chalkidian League was signed, with the blessing of Apollo. The Oracle at Delphi prophesied that the pact would be of value to both, and copies of the document were displayed, not only in the Temple of Apollo at Delphi, but also in the Temple of Artemis at Olynthos, and in the Temple of the Olympian Zeus at Dium, where Philip celebrated Games. Dium was near the coast of eastern Macedonia, south of Pydna, and close to the ancient capital of Aegae.

The excavations at Olynthos have uncovered a very well planned and laid-out city, and the remains of houses and public buildings which line the streets give a good impression of the city as it must have been. The mosaic floors of many of the buildings alone make Olynthos well worth visiting, although they are not quite so fine as those at Pella; and many of the buildings are also of interest.

The end of Olynthos as a city came when Philip, in a situation acerbated by Demosthenes' constant hounding of the king, told the Olynthians that their 'continuance at Olynthos was incompatible with his continuance in Macedonia'. The Athenians hurried troops to the area, but it was too late; and in the late summer of 348 BC Philip captured the town, and wiped out a number of others in the Chalkidiki. Many of the inhabitants of Olynthos were sold into slavery, and the lands, property and captives were divided among leading Macedonians. The final capitulation and almost total destruction of Olynthos was celebrated by Philip with dramatic festivals, Games and feasting on a magnificent scale. The Chalkidiki became then, as it is now, part of Macedonia.

The ancient town of Amphipolis, which is referred to by Herodotus, commanded the foothills of Mount Pangaean, with a fine view across the sea to Mount Athos. It is on the west bank of the river Strymon (Struma) which flows out of Thrace, and which was well-known to Allied armies of the 1914–18 war. At the entrance to the road which leads to the ancient city is the statue of a colossal lion, which was washed down the river, and undoubtedly, at one time, stood within the walls.

As we know from the historian Thucydides there was a bridge across the river from the city at the time of the battle of Amphipolis in 422 BC between Perdiccas, king of Macedonia at that time, and the Spartan Brasidas (Book 4.103–4). Thucydides also remarks that 'the walls did not reach down to it (the river) as they do now'.

Olynthos – Amphipolis

However, we now know from the publication of excavations during 1977 and 1978 that the city wall almost entirely surrounded the group of hills on which the city was built, and that it covered a distance of 7.45 kilometres. In addition, seven towers have been found, standing in dominating positions.

Other walls have also been excavated, and slabbed floors; and a number of cist graves (sepulchral chambers excavated in rock) of the Archaic period have also been found. Earlier in this decade an Archaic Parian inscription was discovered, which may have originated from the colonisers of Thasos, who were Parian.

There is a good sluiced drainage system, and a vast tomb mound, which had burials as early as the Iron Age.

The gateway to the city, built in King Philip's time (the Classical period), has inner and outer courts, and is, as always, an example of the excellence and also beauty of Classical building.

Amphipolis, which was obviously in a key position on the east – west route, to be known by the Roman's as the Via Egnatia, managed, in the main, to preserve its independence until Philip occupied the city in 357 BC, from which time it became a Macedonian city of considerable importance. Its position was vital, situated as it was practically on the slopes of Mount Pangaean with the vast mineral deposits which there were in that area, including much gold; and with a considerable river below, flowing into the sea in a very short distance, east of the Chalkidiki. From it, invasions from the east, particularly from Persia, could be repulsed, and also those from the neighbouring and warlike state of Thrace.

Possession of Amphipolis also meant that the way to Asia and the Black Sea for Philip was now assured. However, it was his son Alexander who made the all-conquering expedition to the east, after his father had been murdered; but it was Philip, and not Alexander, who had prepared the way for the great campaign by the subjugation of Athens.

There is a small museum at Amphipolis, with some pieces of interest on display, but the more important finds from the city, such as the magnificent though broken marble equestrian statue, are in the archaeological museum in Kavala.

Chapter 5

Philippi (Krenides) – Abdera

Original reference to Krenides – later to be called Philippi – is difficult, since it is too late for either Herodotus or Thucydides, although the latter refers to Mount Pangaean, at the foot of which there was so much gold, and near where the city lies. He makes brief reference to the mountain in Book 2, in a sentence which ends 'the whole country is now called Macedonia, and Perdiccas the son of Alexander was the king of it at the time of the invasion of Sitalces ...' This Perdiccas was the father of Archelaos. Later, however, the Thracians recaptured the area, and it was part of Berisades' possessions when Philip II captured Amphipolis, a town of some importance to the west of Mount Pangaean. Berisades, the King of Thrace, died in 357 BC.

In 366 BC, a well-known orator, Kallistratos of Athens, had been accused of treason in that city, and only his brilliant defence of himself at his trial had secured his acquittal. A short time later he was again accused, this time being charged with 'having advised the demos ill ...' and went into exile in Macedonia in approximately 361 BC. Shortly after this he accompanied a party of settlers from the island of Thasos to the district near Neapolis – on the mainland – to prospect for gold. Thasos had suffered a period of occupation which by this time was being relaxed, and a programme of rebuilding had been started, in addition to which they were again minting a limited number of their own coins.

Kallistratos and his party decided to found a Thasian colony slightly to the west of Mount Pangaean, and to prospect for gold in that area. The results were extremely rewarding, and in a short time the mines were yielding fairly large amounts of gold for Thasos, and a small city had been built which was named Krenides.

9 Excavations on main site at Philippi

Kallistratos, ill-advisedly, returned to Athens, only to be executed because of a death sentence which had been passed on him in his absence.

Nonetheless, the mining at Krenides continued, and the mines were yielding considerable quantities by the time of Berisades' death.

Shortly after this, Philip II, who was by then in possession of nearly all eastern Macedonia, not only gave his protection to Thasos, but visited Krenides and took over the gold-mines, considerably increasing the numbers of people working there. After this visit the name of the city was changed to Philippi in his honour; evidence for this is forthcoming from the coinage of the area at that time.

Although the new arrangement was doubtless more advantageous to the king than to Thasos, his considerable power and influence, together with his foresight and organisation, enabled the gold workings to be enormously increased, and before long the mines were producing as much as 1,000 talents a year. Philip appears to have been a generous king, with the wisdom to realise that prosperity in his vassal states and colonies was of much help to his own kingdom, and there is little question that the beautiful city which was built in Thasos during the fourth century BC owed much to the working of the Pangaean gold-mines.

From this source also Philip was enabled to introduce a new gold coinage into Macedonia, based on the stater called after himself, and this, naturally, created a considerable improvement in the economy, as hitherto Persian and Athenian money had been the currency for most of the Greek world.

Much of the timber from the local Pangaean forests was also used for ship-building, and Philip at this time very considerably increased the size of his fleet.

Recent excavation in Philippi, according to reports published in Athens, has revealed a paved street passing in front of the propylaeum of the early church and a 'commercial' road leading to the Neapolis (Kavala) gate, which has now been completely cleared.

10 The theatre at Philippi

Philippi (Krenides) – Abdera

During the 1977 season a sundial made of bronze was found, which dates to the fifth–fourth centuries BC.

The site is very extensive, and as with so many sites in Macedonia, very well placed.

Philippi enjoyed considerable prosperity, not only because of the gold-mines, but also because of its excellent position on the main east–west trade route, the Via Egnatia; and the protection which was given to the city by the surrounding hills. Part of the modern main road still runs over the Via Egnatia.

The remains of the agora are mainly Roman, but on the eastern side of the road are a number of rock-cut tombs of considerably earlier date, and possibly of greater interest to archaeologists, than a great part of the main site where few Archaic and Classical finds have, as yet, been made. The Roman remains are extensive, and there are a number of early Christian churches on the site including a huge fifth century basilica. Philippi was the first European town to be visited by Christian missionaries, in the persons of St. Paul, and Silas who accompanied him, in approximately AD 50.

Of the Roman period, more than one bath establishment has been excavated, and some remarkable latrines; and a number of marble temples and foundations of other buildings have also been found. So much building by the Romans, and later by early Christians and even in the Byzantine era, inevitably damaged, if not ruined, earlier structures, since the marble and stone was frequently used for the newer construction; and even foundations are often difficult to find. This loses for posterity much valuable evidence of earlier civilisations.

The ancient Acropolis is early Macedonian, of the fourth century BC, although there are three towers which are Byzantine, and these can be seen from a considerable distance.

The finds from Philippi are in the museum at Kavala, the ancient city of Neapolis, and this museum is well worth a visit containing, as it does, all of value from the eastern Macedonian sites.

The two great battles between Mark Anthony, and Cassius and Brutus, took place on the plains of Philippi, in 42 BC.

Philippi is fortunate to have had its beautiful theatre already

11 Excavations at Abdera

excavated. This is small by comparison with the great theatres of Dodona and Epidaurus, but considerably larger than many others. It is cut from the eastern hill beyond the tombs, in a semi-circle which is a natural amphitheatre. It was built during the reign of Philip II, but altered later, and was, like many others, a gladiatorial arena during the occupation of the Romans.

Later it was properly restored, and today festivals take place there annually in August and September, when both ancient tragedy and comedy is performed.

Abdera was for a time a possession of Macedonia, but today is just within Thrace. It is on the eastern side of the river Nestos, at its mouth, and has a beautiful coastline and small harbour for fishing boats; the walls of the ancient harbour can still be seen, although now partly under the sea.

It was a flourishing port during the fourth century BC, and it was inevitable that Philip II should have taken it over at this time. He captured Abdera in 354 BC, and, as with all his possessions, it benefited greatly from his kingship.

Herodotus (Book 7.126) refers to the Nestos as 'running through Abdera', and doubtless some part of the port was built further to the west than appears today. It was to Abdera that the Persians under Darius had ordered the Thasian fleet to sail in the previous century.

The city had suffered under Xerxes during the Persian occupation, and Herodotus refers to a citizen called Megacreon telling the people of Abdera to 'take their wives to the temple and tell them to pray heaven to continue to spare them one half of their troubles ... with proper gratitude for the blessing already received that King Xerxes was not in the habit of taking *two* dinners a day'. Thasos at this time also suffered from the rapacious appetites of the Persians.

Abdera was founded during the early Archaic period, but was occupied by colonists from Teos, near Ephesus, in the latter half of the sixth century BC. 'The Teions ... took their ships, and escaped by sea to Thrace – there they founded Abdera ...' (Herodotus, Book 1.170)

Philippi (Krenides) – Abdera

When Philip incorporated Abdera into the kingdom of Macedonia the city was very rich – partly because it had a large port in a valuable position on the east–west sea lanes, which was also a reason for the prosperity of Thasos; and partly because of the very considerable production of corn in the area. It had at one time been the third richest city in the Delian League. In the late fifth century BC the coin types were said to be near perfection; for those interested in the subject there is a valuable book called *The Coinage of Abdera* by J. M. F. May. It is likely that, with the city's expertise and Philip's gold, later pieces were also finely minted and designed.

Most interesting excavations are taking place on the ancient site at Abdera, but photographs are not yet available of that part of the work which is still unpublished. Roman remains cover some extent of this excavation, but the main site, on which work is continuing each year, is of the fifth century BC.

It is thought that the Acropolis is beneath a hill nearby.

Chapter 6

Thasos, Macedonian island

As some grave Tyrian trader from the sea
Described at sunrise an emerging prow
Among the Aegean isles ...
And saw the merry Grecian coaster come
Freighted with amber grapes and 'Thasian' wine
Green bursting figs ...

The island of Thasos was colonised in 680 BC, and became in less than a hundred years the capital city of the area; and only a little later was exporting wine to the whole eastern Mediterranean, and as far afield as Sicily, Egypt, Syria, and even Rome. All wine *amphorae* (two-handled pottery containers with narrow necks) were stamped with a control stamp for export, and these are easily identifiable when excavated. Since the island had a very large wine trade, these stamped amphorae, or pieces of them, have been discovered in many places.

There are some traces of an original occupation of this north Aegean island as early as 1500 BC, and Herodotus refers to a Phoenician invasion of that date in search of gold, but the first certainly known colonisation was by a party from Paros, led by Telesikles, whose grandson was the poet, Archilochos, who lived from approximately 712–664 BC and who invented the iambic metre. The colonisation is dated at 680 BC, and the French School in Athens, who have been responsible for archaeological excavation in the island since 1911, have found much from the Archaic period, particularly in the Artemision.

The *polis* of Thasos was on the north-east side of the island, with excellent sheltered harbours, one of which was a naval dockyard. The city was, and the little modern town still is, completely surrounded by a fortified wall, made of great blocks of (ashlar) marble interspersed with mica-veined gneiss. There are gates at regular intervals in this wall, and fortified towers in between. Much of the existing wall is of the seventh and sixth centuries BC, although some rebuilding took place during the fourth century, together with a certain amount of re-strengthening, which was part of a great programme of building in the city after Philip II of Macedon had rid the country of Athenian power.

The gates are of particular interest, not only to archaeologists, because they are nearly all carved with figures of the ancient Greek gods, in their native, or island, guise. For instance, the two gates between the harbour and the north-east point called Evraiocastro show, on the first a carved horse-drawn chariot led by Hermes, with the goddess Artemis standing in the chariot; and on the second a carving of Hermes, naked, followed by his three attendant Graces.

The first of these gates stands in a small garden full of flowers, which belongs to a present-day Thasian citizen; and the actual gate pillars, which show the opening and closing mechanism very clearly, are in excellent condition.

The Agora, which was always the civic and commercial centre of a Greek city, as well as its market-place, has the remains of many buildings, including temples and porticoes, as well as the bases of a number of statues belonging to Thasian heroes. These include the famous Olympic boxer, Theogenes, who is said to have won 1400 crowns at Games in many places in Greece during his lifetime.

Outside the Agora there are some excavated remains of a sanctuary of the god Dionysos, in which many beautiful objects were found, which are now in the museum, but unhappily there is modern building over much of this site, which of necessity remains largely undug.

Also outside the Agora are the remains of temples to both Herakles and Artemis. The Artemision, in which the buildings are badly shattered, by both earthquake and by removal of stone for later building, has yielded a very large number of valuable finds from its excavation over a number of years. These include some good bronzes, the best of which is an exquisite little figure of the goddess, which had been the handle for a mirror. This is of the seventh century BC. A considerable amount of pottery has also been found on this site, some of which is very lovely, although not the work of sophisticated potters. Thasos had its own pottery workshop, and school of potters, and their output reached its peak during the second half of the seventh century BC. The potters of Thasos continued to work until about 570 BC, when imports from Athens, coupled with increasing prosperity in the island, enabled the islanders to buy pieces from elsewhere and this trade competed too strongly with the island industry.

There is a charming small theatre in Thasos, set in pine-trees above the town, which was originally excavated by two Englishmen, who published their findings in 1887. It is known, from the writings of Hippocrates and others, that this theatre was showing both comedies and tragedies as early as the fifth century BC, and it is also known that there was a season of theatrical productions of particular importance there during the second half of the fourth century BC, probably as a celebration of the island's growing prosperity. After this season, and to commemorate it, five statues were set up in the Sanctuary of Dionysos, and dedicated to the god. They represented Dionysos himself, the Mask of Tragedy, the figure of Comedy, the Dithyramb (the choral song of the cult, and of the tragic theatre) and the Nocturnal Serenade. Some of these figures were excavated, and are now in the museum.

There is still a season of drama in July and August each year, during which ancient Greek plays, both tragic and comic, are performed by the national theatre companies of Greece, and the little theatre is filled to capacity each night.

Local stone must always, particularly on an island, control local building programmes, and the beauty of the buildings on Thasos owes much to the fact that most of the island's natural stone is marble.

In Thasos town, high above the Agora, is the site of the Acropolis, on which stood an enormous temple to Athena, in this case worshipped as Poliouchos – protectress of the city. This temple was made entirely of marble, and its extensive foundations remain.

12 Thasos. Newly excavated gate to the naval dockyard. It was
near this gate that traces of a cult of Philip II as a hero have
been found

Thasos, Macedonian island

When still standing it must have presented a sight more beautiful even than the temples of Segesta and Agrigento, sparkling in the sun above the city. It is just possible to realise how lovely it must have been by climbing to the very top of the Acropolis, and looking at the marble half-column which has been erected there.

The original colonisers, coming as they did from Paros, which is also a marble island, exploited to the full the area of Aliki, in the south of the island. Aliki had natural harbours, and quickly became the centre of the industry, as indeed it still is today. From the sea the cliffs and hills glitter and sparkle for some distance; and the original workings, which are low down by the sea for ease of loading, can still plainly be seen.

Aliki has two small bays, one to the south-east, and one to the south-west, which are divided by a narrow isthmus, and on this isthmus are the remains of two small temples, almost identical in size. This sanctuary was built in the seventh century BC, presumably shortly after the Parian colonisation, and the temples were in constant use until Christianity became the faith of the island.

The original excavation, some seventy-five years ago, was unfortunately carried out without scientific knowledge, or even reasonable care, and not only was much damage done but much valuable information was also lost. However, there are inscriptions on a number of blocks in the sanctuary, wishing safe voyages to the marble-carrying ships; and some of these ships are named, all with the name of a god or goddess of the time. Another interesting inscription which was found recorded thanks to the 'Saviour' or 'Deliverer' gods – the Dioscures – who were the traditional Greek protectors of sailors.

Aliki today is a particularly fascinating place, quite unspoilt by modern development. The south-western bay has fine white sand, and the handful of fishermen's cottages, all of which are built of marble in the old Thasian style with roofs made of marble tiles, stand in a small grove of olive and fig trees, with the great marble quarries above.

Not far from Aliki, near the village of Kinyra, is the district where the gold-mines are supposed to have been. According to

13 Thasos. Gate of the Chariots

Thasos, Macedonian island

Herodotus a Phoenician expedition landed in this area as early as 1500 BC, and in Book 6.47 of the *Histories* he writes:

'I have seen these mines myself – much the most remarkable are those discovered by the Phoenicians, who came with Thasos, the son of Phoenix, to colonise the island which has since borne his name. These Phoenician mines ... lie on the south-eastern side of Thasos, facing Samothrace ...'

There is little, if any, trace of these mines today, but there is some proof of a Phoenician landing on this side of the island in the fact that the French archaeologists found traces of a sanctuary to Melqart, a god identified with Herakles, who was worshipped by natives of Tyre, who were of course Phoenician; and in any case the island was named after Thasos, son of Phoenix. Although gold remains to be discovered, marble is still both quarried and exported, and a large amount is used for building in the island, the chippings being used for paving roads and pathways.

There is a small museum in the town, near the Agora, which contains a number of interesting pieces. From the flourishing school of sculpture which existed in the island during the seventh and sixth centuries BC, there is an immense marble *kouros* carrying a ram; and from the late Classical period, from the school of Praxiteles which was also on the island, there is a marble head of the god Dionysos, which is very beautiful. From the Parian sculptor, Scopas, who also had a school in the island, there is the head of a young man of the mid-fourth century BC, and other pieces from this school have been found. There is some gold, and a little silver and bronze, and also ivories and amber. There is some good pottery of the Archaic period, including a Cycladic plate of the mid-seventh century BC of the Orientalising style; and a plate with a horseman and two black horses, one of which he is riding, while leading the other.

One room contains nothing but pottery made in the Thasian school which was discovered only recently in the Artemision, and here are some fine specimens of flat cups, of which a black one, without figures or other markings, is probably the best.

Thasos, Macedonian island

Excavation is still carried on annually in the island by the French School in Athens (directed by Professor Charles Picard, whose grandfather was one of the earlier excavators), whose publications tell us much about the earlier work. The present day excavations are in association with the Greek Department of Antiquities in Kavala.

Recent excavation has uncovered a fortified gate, leading from the Propylaea of the Agora, and the defensive system which surrounded it. A drain running beneath the fortification still has its original iron grill. This complex is of the early fourth century BC, and it is thought possible that there is another fortified gate on the opposite side, which would have afforded complete protection to the road from the Agora to the harbour and the naval dockyard.

There has also been recent work on the Zeus Gate, and also on the Gate of Silenos; and in the latter area the foundations of a number of buildings are now clear. In addition, a magnificent stretch of the town wall, between this gate and the Gate of the Guardian Gods – Herakles and Dionysos – has been excavated and restored.

As we know, Philip II considerably enlarged the gold workings at Krenides, which was a colony of Thasos; and by reinforcing the team of Thasian workmen there enormously increased the output, thereby benefitting both himself, and the island. In return, Thasos provided Philip with timber for boat building, and the Thasians were, apparently, pleased when the king graciously allowed the name Krenides to be changed to Philippi in his honour. He also gave the island a certain amount of protection. However, throughout the period of our historical knowledge of Thasos, the islanders have always retained their independence of outlook and behaviour, even when the island was occupied, and this independence is noticeable even today.

Thasos is the only inhabited Macedonian island, and, apart from its very interesting antiquities which are visited annually by thousands of people, it is one of the most beautiful of all the Greek islands. A mountain range, which rises to more than 4,000 feet and is extremely well-wooded, ensures a high annual rainfall, which means that even at the height of summer the general appearance is green, when most of Greece and its islands are burnt to a yellowish white.

It is, as yet, largely unexploited commercially, and is therefore unspoilt. It is difficult to know how long this will last, although the conformation of the land, and the comparatively few inhabitants, make industrial development impossible. The main industries are farming, timber, honey and fishing, with the fish mainly going to the port of Kavala each morning. There is also the export of the island's marble, and a certain tourist industry at the height of summer, which is growing; however its main interest lies in the extent and value of its excavations, and this can be realised by the very large number of cultural tours which are run by many countries, in particular from Athens, by the Greeks, the French, the Americans and today by the English and Germans also.

Chapter 7

Cults, rituals and myths

It is reasonable to assume that most of the gods who were worshipped throughout Greece during the Archaic, Classical and Hellenistic pre-Christian periods were also worshipped in Macedonia, although doubtless the worship was more primitive in form in many parts of that mountainous country. Evidence is forthcoming from many of the archaeological sites for most of the cults, although it was often more fashionable to consult the Oracle of Zeus at Dodona than that of Apollo at Delphi.

The royal house of Macedon, particularly in the persons of Philip II and his son Alexander the Great, obviously searched for a religion of the earliest type - a searching after truth in its original form which is forever the longing of thinking mankind; and these two kings were known to have been extremely religious.

The Olympian gods are known only from the sixth century BC, when the Greeks acknowledged Twelve Gods of Mount Olympos with Zeus at their head. Mount Olympos is in Thessaly, just across the southern borders of Macedonia, and many of the Macedonian kings had adherents in Thessaly, and at times owned parts of it.

It would seem that the worship of Zeus in Macedonia was not often that of the civilising influence of Zeus Agoraios, and that the cult of Dionysos was more the cult of Thrace than of Thebes.

In the Archaic and early Classical eras both Epirus and Macedonia, unlike the rest of Greece, consisted of a number of tribes of mainly peasant people, working on the land and tending their sheep and goats; and these tribes owed allegiance to, and were held together by, their kings, unlike the position in the *polis* or city-state which had become almost universal in the rest of the country. For this reason the royal house of Macedon and Epirus found that union in marriage, as well as co-operation in other ways, was useful

Cults, rituals and myths

to both. That they were divided by the Pindus mountains, a range which rises in places to more than 7,000 feet, does not seem to have interfered with this arrangement, and the barrier was obviously useful at the times when they were not in accord with each other.

Zeus is the only Greek god whose Indo-European background can be claimed with certainty, and in Greece his oldest known shrine is at Dodona, where his consort was Dione – variously referred to as the 'Earth-mother', or as the feminine version of Zeus. Such details of this cult as are known will be dealt with in the chapter on Dodona. There are, of course, sanctuaries of the later cults of Zeus in a number of places in Macedonia, and many different myths are associated with these shrines.

On vases Zeus is generally shown as a dignified figure with a pointed beard. As the supreme sky-god, he is often shown with his thunderbolt. Many bronze statues, of all sizes, of Zeus have been excavated, the largest and probably the most famous being in the National Museum in Athens. The god is shown with arms outstretched, about to hurl his thunderbolt from his right hand, but the thunderbolt was missing when this statue was recovered from the sea near Cape Artemision. This bronze is of the early Classical period, and has the usual pointed beard, and an expression of calm and serenity as befits a god of the sky. The whole figure gives an immense impression of strength and power.

A beautiful bronze of Zeus was also excavated at Dodona. This too has a pointed beard, and arms outstretched, but in this case the thunderbolt – a cigar-shaped object – had not been lost, and is held in the right hand. This statue, which is, sadly, in the Staatliche Museum in Berlin, is also of the early Classical period.

Zeus was always the protector of law and morals, although his loves were many, and varied, and he fathered numerous children. His wife was the goddess Hera, herself one of the Olympic Twelve. Importance is attached to the story of Zeus' birth in a cave in Crete, after which he was hidden to prevent his father Kronos from swallowing him as he had already done with other of his children. There is also a claim for the god's birthplace being in Arcadia – near Olympia.

Cults, rituals and myths

Zeus was worshipped in many forms, and in a country of mainly peasant peoples, such as Macedonia, it is almost certain that the forms of Zeus-Herkeios (of the courtyard), and Zeus-Ktesios (of the household) were much in evidence, and that the ritual of the cult was adapted by the priests to suit the peoples concerned.

In the pre-historical age Homer had impressed the image of the god upon the Greeks, but inevitably later the myths and rituals varied according to the district, and newer gods, particularly Dionysos, attracted the Macedonian people.

Among others of the Olympian pantheon with whom we are concerned is a brother of Zeus – Poseidon, the god of earthquakes, and water, and the sea. Hesiod in the *Theogony* says he was older than Zeus, although Homer refers to him as being the younger of the two.

In a country such as Macedonia with a considerable sea-coast Poseidon must necessarily have had many shrines. Homer mentions him in connection with Aegae, and in one passage claims that the god could reach this place with four strides from Samothrace (*Iliad*, 13). The God had sat down on the topmost peak of Samothrace to watch the battle between Hector and the Trojans and 'the ships of the Achaeans (Greeks) could also be seen'; and then '... he made three stides, and with the fourth reached Aegae ...' where his famous palace, built in gleaming gold, stood. Is this the ancient capital of Macedonia? or the Aegae of Herodotus, which is in the Pelopponese, in the district known as Achaea? Only time will show, but the former makes more sense, though it should be remembered that Homer always refers to the Greeks as Achaeans.

Among the myths of Poseidon, his fathering of Pegasos with the gorgon Medusa is interesting, and there are other tales of his siring of horses. In Archaic and Classical art this god is usually shown with a trident; the earlier vases show him clothed, but later he is nearly always naked. His association with earthquakes could have arisen from the pseudo-scientific idea that earthquakes were, in some unexplained manner, caused by the movement of water.

Poseidon's association with horses doubtless came from the first invasion of the Hyksos people, Indo-Europeans who were known as the shepherd-kings of the east (Gardiner, *Egypt of the Pharaohs* p. 148), who brought not only their horses but also their gods to Greece with them. According to Farnell, the cult of Poseidon Hippios is peculiarly Thessalian.

Some mention must also be made of Demeter, one of the older goddesses of Mount Olympos desired by Zeus. 'Demeter, who feeds all, came to the bed of Zeus, and bore white-armed Persephone ...' Demeter was a daughter of Rhea, who, according to Hesiod, '... being forced by Kronos, bore him most brilliant children ...' She was the great corn-goddess of Greece, and is, of course, best known for the cult of Demeter at Eleusis, and the Eleusinian Mysteries. The Great Mysteries were held in early autumn, when life was returning to the land after the droughts of summer and the accompanying barrenness of the fields and hills; and the Lesser Mysteries were connected with the spring, when the 'young' corn, or seed, was under the earth. These mysteries were associated with death, and re-birth, not only of the corn, but also with the hope of human immortality. Little is known of the rituals, which were older than the cult of Demeter, and the true facts of this mystery religion are still very obscure.

Many are the myths surrounding the daughter of Demeter's union with Zeus. Persephone, or Kore as she is known in Greece, appears on the wall-painting of one of the newly-discovered tombs at Vergina. The myth of her visit to the Underworld and subsequent imprisonment there is too well-known to be repeated here, but it is extremely old, and the Homeric hymn to Demeter describes it in poetic language. A comment on this hymn observes 'Though we now read this hymn as pleasing poetry, to the Eleusinians for whom it was composed it was genuine and sacred history.'

The Homeric hymn is a long one, vividly written, and there is a lovely description of the goddess in it, part of which is worth quoting.

> ... I am honoured Demeter, who is the greatest benefit and joy to immortals and mortals. But come, let all the people build

for me a great temple, and under it an altar, below the city and the lofty wall ... thus having spoken, the goddess changed her magnitude and mien, having put off old age, and beauty was breathed around her, and a pleasant odour was scattered from her scented clothes, and far gleamed the light from the immortal flesh of the goddess, and her yellow curls flourished on her shoulders and the close dwelling was filled with the sheen, as of lightning.

In Classical as well as Archaic art Demeter is shown with a sceptre and ears of corn, and Kore is frequently with her.

Many of the other gods were worshipped in Macedonia, too numerous to mention separately here, but there were three more who were of particular importance. The first of these is Hermes, another of the Olympic Twelve – messenger and bearer of tidings, and in particular the winged messenger of the great god, Zeus, whose son he was. He is referred to as 'silver-tongued', which seems to mean a lack of moral integrity and development. His oldest cult appears to have been connected with fertility, as most of them were, and with this cult his emblem was just a phallos. He is said to have invented the art of fire-making, and was frequently worshipped in the areas of the more primitive peoples. However, his main function later was as the messenger of the gods, particularly of Zeus, and in this capacity he is shown wearing the *petasos*, the broad hat normally worn by Greek travellers; a cloak and sandals; and carrying the *kerykeion*. In Archaic and Classical art his sandals were winged, and in the Archaic period he was frequently shown wearing a *chiton*, and with a pointed beard.

His name is connected with stones, or a stone; and with the herms (stones or marbles with a human head) so prevalent in pre-Christian Greece. Homer (*Odyssey*, 24.1) refers to him as the guide of souls, and as carrying 'a beautiful golden rod, with which he soothes the eyes of men'.

There is an Homeric hymn dedicated to him, of some length, in which his birth is described:

... the beneficial messenger of the immortals whom Maia

brought forth . . . her cunning son, of fair speech, a thief, a stealer
of cattle, an escorter of dreams, a looker-out for night . . . Born
at dawn, he played the lyre at midday, in the evening he stole
the cows of the far-darting Apollo, on the fourth day of the
month, on which his mother Maia gave him birth . . .

Whoever wrote the Homeric hymns, be it one poet or many,
has left for mankind most vivid descriptions of the ancient gods
of Greece.

As a herald Hermes had to speak well to enable him to present
the business on which he had been sent, and in time he became,
according to Homer in particular, a patron of literature. He is
represented in carvings of the Archaic and Classical eras, and in
Macedonia – particularly in Thasos – he is sometimes shown with
the accompanying Graces, or Charities. In this Macedonian island,
in the Passage of the *theoroi* which is just without the Agora,
Hermes – in a carved relief which was excavated during the 1860's,
and taken to the Louvre – is shown sharing an altar with the god
Apollo. This would have been the island representation of
Hermes, who is also carved on two of the gates, welcoming the
visiting god from Delphi. The sharing of an altar, even though
the officiating priests must have sacrificed from opposite sides, is
most unusual, and some archaeologists say that this sanctuary is
unique in Greece. Instructions for sacrifice were carved above the
niche in which the altar stood, and appear to oppose each other, but
there was only one altar.

Hermes was also carved, with Zeus, on one of the pillars of the
main gate of the city of Thasos. Only fragments of this pillar remain, and are in the museum there, although the opposite pillar – of
Hera, and her messenger Iris – still stands and is in good condition.

Herakles, both as god and hero, was intimately connected with
the royal house of Macedon, and the Macedonian kings claimed
descent from Zeus through him. As a hero his many labours are
well-known, and are variously described, but probably most accu-
rately as mythological representation of the overcoming of human
evils by man, through divine inspiration.

Cults, rituals and myths

A very beautiful Homeric hymn to his birth exists which starts 'I will sing Herakles – the son of Zeus whom Alkmene bore, the most valiant of earthly beings, in Thebes of beauteous quires, having been embraced by dark-clouded Zeus.'

Herakles was the most famous of all the Greek heroes, and was ultimately deified by burning himself on his own funeral pyre, and thus attaining immortal status.

In archaeological excavation endless argument takes place as to whether the temples dedicated to Herakles were concerned with him as god or hero. If hero, then the sacrifice would have been made with a sunken hearth – in other words a pit – into which the head of the animal would have been held down, and its blood would have fallen. If god, then the sacrifice would have been on a raised altar, with the animal's head held upwards.

In this book we are particularly concerned with the fact that Herakles was one of the gods to whom Philip II regularly sacrificed, and when Isocrates wrote his famous *Philippos* he hailed Philip as a descendant of Herakles.

Professor Rose describes Herakles as the common property of the entire Greek race, and there is no doubt that his cult was widespread. There are references in Herodotus to very ancient cults of Herakles, and he refers to a temple on Thasos built by the Phoenicians '. . . and even this was five generations before Herakles, the son of Amphitryon, made his appearance in Greece'. In another place he remarks '. . . the result of these researches is a plain proof that the worship of Herakles is very ancient'.

Herakles was a son of Zeus and the beautiful Alkmene, who is said to have lain first with Zeus, who appeared to her in the guise of her betrothed husband, Amphitryon; and later on the same night with Amphitryon himself. From these two unions Alkmene bore twins, one of whom was human, one half-man, half-god.

There is an interesting theory propounded by Professor Rose and others that the Herakles hero-myth had foundations in the person of a real nobleman who inhabited the great palace of Tyrins in Mycenean days.

Herakles is shown on Macedonian coins, often as an archer. Good examples of them were found by the French archaeologists on Thasos, where there is a sanctuary to the god mentioned by Herodotus, and also more than once by Hippocrates.

During the early part of the Archaic period a new deity swept through Greece, though there are many and varied records of this god hundreds of years earlier in Egypt, and in many other places round the eastern Mediterranean.

Dionysos, son of Zeus, and a mortal woman, Semele, became for Thrace, and later for Macedonia as well as many other parts of Greece, a god who could produce overwhelming religious fervour, sometimes mystic, sometimes orgiastic, but always demanding all from his adherents.

This, most fascinating of all the pre-Christian Greek gods, has driven scholars almost to despair in their desire to discover more of the underlying beauty and mystery of his cult. And yet for this god there is a first-hand record in Euripides' incomparable play, the *Bacchae*, which was written when Dionysos' hold on Greece was at the height of its power, and when his worship was particularly strong in Macedonia.

Dionysos appears as Cretan, Phrygian, Egyptian (Herodotus, Book 11) and Thracian, and he is mentioned by Homer, although his appeal was not for the Homeric knights. However, there is a charming Homeric hymn to this god, number XXIV, which starts 'I begin to sing ivy-crowned, roving Dionysos, the glorious son of Zeus and renowned Semele, whom the fair-haired nymphs receiving him from his royal sire in their bosoms, nurtured and brought up assiduously in the valleys of Nysa. But he grew up under the care of his sire in a fragrant sweet-smelling cave, being numbered among the immortals ...' There is also another, longer Homeric hymn to this god.

Many of the earlier accounts appear to contradict each other about him. As told in the *Bacchae*, violent retribution overtook Pentheus, king of Thebes and mythologically related to the god through his mother, for his opposition to the new cult; and the manifestation of Dionysiac power to the Argive women was even worse.

Cults, rituals and myths

The cult is decribed as often wild and violent, but doubtless this was, as explained by Professor Rose, 'but an idealization of the enthusiastic ritual of the god'.

His followers were known as *Bakchoi*; the cult was an emotional religion, more concerned with fertility and regeneration than with wine, although the unsealing and tasting of the new wine formed part of the ritual of the Anthesteria. Three festivals were connected with Dionysos – Anthesteria, Lenaea and Dionysia, the last of which was a religious-dramatic festival – and his worship also inspired countless other small celebrations throughout Greece. With the ever-growing interest in drama, Dionysia were held everywhere, and at the Greater City Dionysia, held annually in Athens, the poets competed against each other with their plays. Tragedy was not ritual drama, but its associations with religion were there from the beginning.

The Greater Dionysia was a magnificent festival, on a very large scale. On the first day there was a spectacular ceremonial procession to escort the cult-statue of Dionysos to the theatre, which still stands below the Acropolis in Athens, after which a bull was sacrificed to the god. This was followed by a competition of dithyrambic odes by choruses of fifty, accompanied by flutes. There were ten of these choruses, five composed of men, and five of boys. Euripides, the author of ninety tragic plays, including the *Bacchae* which he wrote in Macedonia, did not win a chorus until 455 BC (he was born in about 484 BC), and his *Peliades* was performed in Athens that year.

The second day of the festival was taken up with the production of comedies, after which there were three days of tragedies competing for the prizes.

The satyrs who danced in the *thiasos* or revel rout of Dionysos were frequently shown as being half-man, half-goat. *Tragos* means a goat, from which tragedy derived its name.

The understanding of tragedy, with its underlying beauty, pathos and horror, is hard, but Professor Albin Lesky, in his superb book *Greek Tragedy*, seems to convey something of its real meaning. In a fascinating chapter entitled 'What is Tragedy?' he discusses

75

the subject from many angles, and one sentence, which is a quotation from Hebbel, seems to sum up the tragic concept: '... deeply embedded in the world are opposing forces which spell conflict and annihilation to anyone who finds himself between the two fronts ... this tragic conflict reaches deep into God's essential nature ...' And so we have the opposing forces in the Dionysiac cult – the beauty and the horror; the desire for true mystic ecstasy, for the ability to lift man out of himself and above the cares and tribulations of his ordinary life; and the sometimes orgiastic and horrifying interpretation of the rituals.

Euripides, living at the height of the cult in Macedonia, writes of the god describing himself in inimitable words: '... Dionysos son of Zeus, consummate god – most terrible, and yet most gentle to mankind.'

In Macedonia the cult gained very considerable ground, and many beautiful archaeological finds bear witness to this fact, of which the pebble mosaic of the god and his panther at Pella, and the Praxiteles' head of the god found in the Dionysion in Thasos, are two of the more remarkable; and the Derveni vase, in the museum in Thessaloniki, is wholly concerned with the god and his followers, as will be seen in Chapter 9.

Chapter 8

The cult and Oracle of Dodona

For an understanding of pre-Christian Greece it is very necessary to realise how large a part was played by religious cults in the every-day life of every citizen, be he king or peasant. No enterprise or expedition was undertaken without previous sacrifice to a god, or gods; votive (dedicated or consecrated) offerings were made to gods and goddesses, petitioning for help or giving thanks for benefits received – particularly for fertility. The great dramatic fes-tivals which took place annually throughout Greece, and especially tragedy (although it was not the ritual of a cult), were nonetheless closely associated with religion from their beginnings; and the priest of the cult of Dionysos usually had a seat in the theatre. Every aspect of life had its god or goddess; there were twelve gods of Mount Olympos, known as the Great Gods; there were protecting gods; gods of animals; of the sea; and of the air. All drinking, whether ceremonial or informal, started with the act of 'pouring a libation for the god', and certain excavations, such as that of the Palace of Nestor at Pylos in the Peloponnese, have revealed channels cut in the floor – at Pylos beside the throne – into which the libations were poured.

In Hesiod's *Theogony*, and also in *Works and Days*, which is a magnificent poem, we have a very complete picture of the ancient Greek conception of the origin of the world, the birth of the gods and much superstitious lore; combined with agricultural advice, and political and social comment. From the evidence available Hesiod lived at the end of the eighth century BC, was a contemporary of Homer and was a native of Boeotia on the Greek mainland.

One of the oldest known sanctuaries in Greece, and the oldest known Oracle, is that of Zeus and the 'Earth mother' at Dodona. Philip of Macedon had considerable connections with this place, as did his son Alexander the Great; and particularly his queen, Olympias.

Dodona is not in Macedonia, but in the contingent state of Epirus. Epirus was ruled by the Molossian royal house of the Aeacidae. As we have seen in Chapter 1, the Molossian king gave his daughter Olympias to Philip of Macedon to be his queen in gratitude for Philip's great victory in 358–7 BC over the Illyrians who occupied the country to the north of both Macedonia and Epirus. Their defeat relieved the immense pressure that Illyria had exerted against Epirus. About ten years later Philip made an expedition against Epirus and its then king Arybbas, after which, according to Pickard-Cambridge (*Cambridge Ancient History*), he became the 'virtual master of a great part of Epirus'. Some years later he assisted Olympias' brother, Alexander, of the Molossian royal house, to become king of the state, and further to cement the two states, in 336 BC, he gave his daughter by Olympias to Alexander as his bride. It was at the festivities held in honour of this wedding that he was murdered.

The Oracle of Zeus at Dodona was consulted by numbers of people from many parts of Greece, and during much of Philip's reign it was fashionable to consult the Oracle there. Whether Philip himself ever visited Dodona is uncertain, though likely. Had he required to consult the Oracle he would, of course, have despatched religious envoys with the question, and would not have gone in person. However, the recent excavations of the royal burials at Vergina make it appear likely that, whoever was the owner of the unplundered tomb – in fact of both unplundered tombs – had some link with the Dodonian cult. In both, the caskets containing the cremated remains were covered with branches of oak and with acorns, and in the tomb discovered in the 1978 season the burial had taken place so hastily that some of the acorns were found outside the door.

Dodona lies a short distance south of Ioannina, in magnificent mountain scenery. It is a country of shepherds, ilex and cornfields, and the actual site is in a long narrow valley, of great beauty. There is an interesting fragment of a lost poem of Hesiod, called *Eoiai*

14 Bouleuterion and wall of theatre at Dodona

which was written during the eighth century BC, and after more than 2500 years the description of the area could have been written today. 'Hellopia was a country of cornfields and meadows, abounding in sheep and oxen, and inhabited by numerous shepherds and keepers of cattle, where on an extremity stood Dodona, beloved by Zeus. Here the god established his Oracle, in a wood of ilex.'

The original shrine of the Oracle probably existed before 2000 BC, and was dedicated to the 'Earth-mother' or goddess. This was a cult of southern Greece which had, like the cult of Zeus, originated in the east. Archaeological finds date from the Early Bronze Age, approximately 2500 BC, and are in the museum in Ioannina. There is a mention of the shrine by Homer, in the *Iliad*, which is the earliest reference known, in which Achilles fetches the cup which he kept for libations to no other god but Zeus. After ritual cleansing of the cup, which included fumigation with sulphur, and rinsing in 'a rill of fresh water', he washed his hands, and drew some sparkling wine. Then, going to the forecourt to pray, he said 'Dodonian Pelasgian Zeus – you that live far away and rule over wintry Dodona, surrounded by your prophets the Helli – who leave their feet unwashed, and sleep upon the ground ...' The Helli, or Selli as they were sometimes called, were the priests of the Dodonian cult, who interpreted the sayings of the Oracle. The answers to questions were transmitted in two forms; either by the rustling of the oak leaves in the sanctuary of Zeus, or by the Helli hitting a number of bronze tripods arranged in a circle, also within the sanctuary.

As always we have a graphic description from Herodotus of the founding of the shrine of the Oracles at Dodona, in Book 2.55–56.

According to the priests of the Theban Zeus, two women connected with the service of the temple were carried off by the Phoenicians and sold ... At Dodona, the priestesses who deliver the Oracles have this version of the story. Two doves (or grey pigeons) flew from Thebes in Egypt (Luxor) and one of them alighted at Dodona ...

15 Sanctuary of Zeus, with oak tree. Dodona, below Mount
Tomarus

The cult and Oracle of Dodona

Then Herodotus adds an explanation of his own:

'personally I would suggest that if the Phoenicians really carried off women from the temple ... the one who was brought to Greece, or Pelasgia as it was then called, must have been sold, and later when she was working as a slave at Dodona she built, under an oak, a shrine to Zeus. Subsequently, when she learned to speak Greek, she established an Oracle there. The story which the people of Dodona tell about the doves, I should say, came from the fact that the woman was foreign, and her language sounded like the twittering of birds; and when, later on, the dove spoke with a human voice, it was because the woman had learned to talk intelligibly ...'

The site at Dodona, which is in a magnificent setting, is very extensive, and it was only discovered comparatively late. In the 1830s Christopher Wordsworth wrote 'The former dwelling-place of the spirit (Dodona) which once guided half the world, is lost ...' However, in 1895, after soundings and excavations had been carried out, the present site was established as Dodona, but the great theatre, which is surely the most lovely in Greece, was only finally cleared and restored between 1960 and 1963. A considerable season of both tragedy and comedy is now held there each summer.

Immediately beyond the theatre are the remains of the meeting house of the representatives of Dodona, known as the 'Bouleuterion', which was built at much the same time as the theatre, by the king Pyrrus (297–272 BC) during the early Hellenistic period.

All the ancient sanctuaries are beyond, in a grove of ilex and olive trees.

Two distinct cults were connected with the Oracle; that of the oriental 'Earth-mother' Gaia; and that of the Indo-European Zeus. Gaia's sacred symbols were the pigeon, the bull, the boar and the double-headed axe; the symbol of Zeus here was the oak-tree, which was sacred to the god and the instrument of his Oracle; and there is no other Oracular oak-tree in Greece. The cult had nothing to do with the Aegean tree cult. The cults at Dodona are known

16 Ancient sanctuary of goddess Dione at Dodona

to have existed as early as the fourteenth–thirteenth centuries BC, and probably before, and three superimposed cult layers have been found. The earliest of these, of the late third–early second millenia BC, proved existence of worship of the pre-Greek earth goddess, later known as Gaia, who represented fertility in all things. When, in the early part of the second millenium BC, the Thesproti tribe migrated to Epirus, they brought their own Indo-European cult with them – that of the oak tree – and later the oak became the place of the goddess, which can be proved from finds of seals and rings of the Mycenaean period in the area, on which this is shown. Finally, the Greek god, Zeus, came to be worshipped at Dodona, and the 'Earth-goddess' became his consort, and adopted the feminine form of his name – Dione.

Early in the fourth century BC the Molossi took over Dodona, and found the priests of the cult, the Helli, still with 'unwashed feet, and sleeping on the ground'. At this time Zeus and Dione were thought to dwell either at the roots of the sacred oak, or on the magnificent mountain Tomarus, above Dodona.

Until the end of the fifth century BC, Zeus had been worshipped in the open air, beneath the oak tree in the sanctuary, and numbers of cauldrons and tripods stood round the oak to protect it. In answer to questions to the Oracle, the Helli struck the cauldrons, and then interpreted the will of the god.

Questions to the Oracle were inscribed on lead, and a very large number of these have been excavated, and can be seen in Ioannina museum; and fascinating indeed are some of the questions asked. From the late sixth–early fifth century BC comes the request 'To which god should he pray in order to do what he has in his mind?' (plate 18). An undated lead has the inscription 'Whether it is all right to buy the small lake by the Sanctuary of Demeter?' This incidentally proves the existence of a sanctuary of Demeter on the site. On one of those leads which were inscribed at the time of Philip II of Macedon we read 'Am I her children's father?' and another, of the fourth century, requests 'Has Pistos stolen the wool from the mattress?' Some with answers given by the Helli have also been found, such as 'Timodamos asks Zeus if he should engage in

17 Bronze figure of boy with a pigeon or dove. Hellenistic
period – from Dodona

trade by land and sea with the money from his silver mine?', to which he gets a very positive reply: 'He should stay in the city, and engage in trade there.' This looks as if the Helli were not wholly disinterested.

Among the remains are two shrines to Dione; a new temple and the foundations of an older one. In front of these is the temple of Zeus, which has well-built walls; an altar; and an inner sanctuary, which would have contained the cult-statue of the god. There is also an oak tree growing within the walls, as there always has been. There are also remains of sanctuaries – mainly foundations – of Aphrodite, Herakles, Apollo, Themis and Dionysos, which are mainly of the third century BC.

The Oracle at Dodona remained until the fourth century AD, and during the following century a Christian basilica with three aisles was built, of which there are extensive remains.

In the fine modern museum in Ioannina one whole room is filled with the finds from Dodona, and, continuing the association of pigeons or doves with the site, there is a very lovely small bronze of a naked boy, holding a dove, of the Hellenistic period. There is some gold, and some beautiful bronzes, of which the model of a lion, and the statuette of a warrior, both of the Archaic period, are of note; and of considerable interest are the bronze legs of a number of the tripods of the Oracle, of the eighth century BC, the geometric period. The finest bronze which has to date been excavated, that of a Laconian girl running, of approximately 550 BC, is in the National Museum in Athens. There is also a lovely little bronze of a priestess, pouring wine from a jug into a cup, in the Louvre in Paris. This is also of the Archaic period. However, the bronze eagle, which probably crowned the sceptre of Zeus held by the cult statue, is in Ioannina. This is 500–450 BC.

Hanging on the wall in the Dodonian room at Ioannina is one of the 'round shields of the Macedonians', and there are also coins from Pella, and other coins which are of Macedonian minting, some of which bear Philip's head or his chariot.

Queen Olympias is known to have taken a great interest in the Oracle, and was active in protest at any interference from Athens

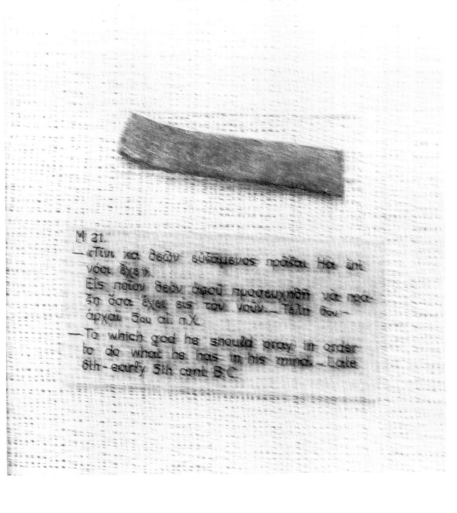

18 Request to the Oracle at Dodona, inscribed on lead (with translation)

The cult and Oracle of Dodona

in Dodonian affairs. Later, when her son Alexander the Great had succeeded Philip as king of Macedonia, they planned to re-build some of the sanctuaries at Dodona, on a far more magnificent scale. This plan was not put into effect until the reign of the Molossian Pyrrus, who introduced the Herakles cult, and built a temple to that god; and finally a programme of re-building was carried out jointly between Epirus and Macedonia, after 218 BC, by Philip V of Macedon. In the new building scheme, the sacred oak in the Zeus sanctuary was 'enclosed by a colonnade, in the shape of an open rectangle' (Dakaris). Philip V of Macedonia had acquired the funds for this re-building by the capture of Thermum.

Today, a visit to Dodona from Macedonia is an extremely reward-ing experience, particularly if undertaken during the spring or early summer. It necessitates driving over the excellent new road across the Pindus mountains, with breath-taking views nearly the whole way; and finally, the short drive from Ioannina, with the road winding up an easy hill suddenly to arrive in a pastoral valley of great beauty with giant mountains towering overhead, is a fitting preparation for the strange atmosphere – which is not only of age and of peace, but of being above and almost out of the world – which surrounds this oldest Oracle of the gods.

Chapter 9

Thessaloniki – the Archaeological Museum

The capital city of Macedonia, Thessaloniki, is situated at the head of the Themaic Gulf, with a large harbour, and a beautiful sea front. It is the second largest city in Greece, and is accessible from both eastern and western Macedonia.

Founded in 315 BC by Cassander, who was a general in the army of Alexander the Great, it has no buildings earlier than the Hellenistic period (323–27 BC) and it did not, in fact, become Macedonia's capital city until after the Roman occupation in 168 BC.

For the student of Byzantine art and of early Christian churches, it is of much interest; and the round Church of St. George, which has also at times served as a mosque, is of particular note.

Thessaloniki was named after Cassander's wife, who was a sister of Alexander the Great; and after the harbour at Pella silted up it became the chief port of Macedonia, and has remained so ever since.

Under the Romans the city became a free state, and it was undoubtedly extremely prosperous as is shown by the prolific coinage of that time.

The Archaeological Museum, which houses much of the magnificent treasure which has been excavated from sites in many places in Macedonia, is near the centre of the modern town, and not far from the well-known landmark of the White Tower, which was built by Venetians.

The museum is in a fine position with large gardens in front, and was one of the first to be built in Macedonia after the liberation of Northern Greece in 1912.

With all archaeological excavation, pottery finds are the most important as they enable accurate dating to be made, and Macedonian

finds contain sherds and pieces which date back to the Protogeometric period, a style which was created in Athens in approximately the eleventh century BC. To quote R. M. Cook, until recently Laurence Professor of Classical Archaeology in the University of Cambridge, 'Macedonia ... had imported Mycenaean
(pottery) but retained its native tradition. That tradition continued
in the Iron Age, but at some time Protogeometric style took root
beside it ...' From the excavations which take place annually,
hundreds of thousands of sherds are recovered from this period
onwards, which include Geometric – early, middle and late; Corinthian of the seventh–sixth centuries BC; Thasian from the pottery
workshop on that island; and later much that is of Athenian (Attic)
and of more sophisticated origin.

In the Thessaloniki museum there are also finds from Macedonia
and Thrace of the pre-historic period, particularly neolithic pottery
from Paradimi in Thrace; and finds from the cemetery at Vergina
dating to the Iron Age, briefly described in Chapter 2, and there
are also two vases of Mycenaean style (1400–1100 BC) although
they may be later in origin. Finds from Olynthos are also displayed in the museum.

There is some sculpture of the Archaic period (720–480 BC) and
later, but the greatest possessions are from the golden age of the
Classical era, the fourth century BC, and also from the later Hellenistic period, and here are a number of pieces of real magnificence,
which compare with anything so far found in the world. The recent
finds at Vergina, excavated by Professor Andronicos and his team,
must rank as the most important to be made in Greece since the
Tomb of Agamemnon was opened by Heinrich Schliemann at
Mycenae and found to be full of gold treasure, including the
famous Mask; which finds were published by Schliemann in 1878 –
just one hundred years before. The Vergina finds will, as far as is
yet possible, be dealt with at the end of this chapter.

During the comparatively recent construction of the Thessaloniki–Kavala road, tombs of the fourth century BC were found
at a place called Derveni, ten kilometres from Thessaloniki. The
tombs were intact, and the treasures from them now fills one whole

room in the museum. Of this treasure the outstanding piece is a bronze krater, entirely adorned with carvings, and with the words 'Asteioios, son of Anaxogoros of Larissa' engraved on it, which was presumably the name of the owner. It is of interest that Larissa is in Thessaly, which at times paid tribute to Philip II, and also to King Antigonos Gonatos. The krater dates to approximately 330 BC, the late Classical period. The sides are decorated with reliefs of maenads and satyrs ecstatically dancing round the god Dionysos and his wife Ariadne; and there are vine-leaves entwined above their heads. On the shoulders of the krater are four figures – on one side a maenad and Dionysos; on the other another maenad, this time with a satyr. Two snakes, also emblems of the Dionysos cult, are coiled around the handles of the krater, and a head – possibly that of Herakles – is inset in both. The figure of Dionysos is thought to be the work of the great sculptor from the island of Paros, Scopas, who also had a workshop on Thasos.

Many other silver and bronze objects were found at Derveni and are on display, including amphorae; oinochoe (wine-pourer jugs) and cups – in particular a flat bronze cup, with wide handles; and also a silver wine-strainer, exquisitely decorated round its rim. Both these pieces are of the late fourth century BC.

Among many other things in this room which are worthy of mention is a faience vase. This is Hellenistic, and was made in Egypt. It shows the goddess Artemis in the midst of a forest, and a number of wild animals are with her. This vase was found in a tomb in the Thessaloniki area, as were a number of gold medals, and pieces of jewellery. There are also some mosaics, with glass tesserae, but these in no way equal the pebble mosaics of Pella, Olynthos and Room 13 in the palace at Vergina. However, it is from Vergina, from the great tumulus, that the spectacular treasure of the royal tombs of the Macedonian kings has come.

There is now little doubt that one of these tombs is that of King Philip II; and there is evidence for this in a number of things. The date of the tomb is right, and the cremated bones are those of a man of between forty and fifty years old, and it is known that Philip was forty-six years old when he was killed. A pair of leather greaves was excavated, with metal bands, and one of these was shorter than the other. It is, of course, well known that Philip was lame, from a severe leg-wound which he sustained when subduing the Illyrians in 344 BC. Like everything else which was discovered, this pair of greaves was photographed in situ before anything was touched by the archaeologists.

Five small masks were found, one of which is an easily recognisable likeness to the head of the king reproduced on a coin found in Thasos by the French excavators there. In both Philip is shown with one blind eye – his eye had been put out with a spear during the siege of Methone★. It is unlikely that more certain proof will be forthcoming, owing to the obvious difficulties with all cremated remains, but the majority of scholars feel that this tomb is that of Philip of Macedon, although the excavators are not prepared to insist on this fact – at any rate as yet.

The contents of the tombs at Vergina however are of a magnificence which is difficult of description. Some pieces are already cleaned and on view in the museum, but when everything is there the exhibition will equal other gold treasure from any excavation in the world.

The two gold caskets from the second tomb to be opened were both in marble containers. One was smaller than the other, but both were entirely of gold, with the radiating star of Macedonia on each lid, and gold repoussé rosettes on the sides. In the large casket, above the cremated remains, was a gold filigree semi-circular jewel, of oakleaves and acorns, exquisitely wrought. A gold head of Medusa was found, with the snakes on her hair made in gold, and this piece was in magnificent condition. Many silver spear-heads were in the tomb, and one of gold, underlining the well-known fact that the 'long spears of the Macedonians brought terror to their opponents'.

There is a wine-strainer, made in gold and silver, which is 4 drachmae in weight, and there is a considerable number of gold and silver cups and jugs of many types, including a flat silver cup with wide handles, which is not unlike the bronze cup from Derveni.

★ This coin is now in the Biblioteque Nationale de Paris.

A gold quiver was found, magnificently carved, with two rows of raised figures – one row consisting of bowmen, with bows and arrows. The Macedonians did not use bows and arrows, neither did the Greeks, and it is thought that this piece, which is in very fine condition, could be Scythian. Philip made an expedition against Ateas, the king of the Scythian tribes, in 339 BC, but was attacked by a wild Balkan tribe known as the Triballi on his return journey, and both he and his forces were robbed of most of their booty. It is therefore likely that this quiver was being worn, possibly by the king, and was therefore not stolen. It is a remarkable piece of gold carving, and unique in Greece.

Another piece of much interest is a leather corselet which is decorated on the front with six lion's heads of solid gold.

A large, vase-like metal object, made of silver and gold, with pierced sides caused the archaeologists some questioning as to its use until it was realised that a terra cotta lamp fitted inside it, which when lit gave a diffused light through the holes. This is a very unusual piece, and there was also a gold and silver torch, which had the flame partially enclosed. Both these pieces are of obviously great interest.

With so much of beauty and magnificence, it would be difficult to itemise the most beautiful, but many people would agree that their choice would be a gold filigree diadem, exquisitely made. The jewel is made of gold wire, super-imposed with leaves of myrtle made in gold, and coloured flowers made of jewels. On two of these flowers are minute gold bees, correct in every detail, and in the centre is a tiny gold bird, of very perky appearance. This is truly a diadem fit for a queen, and doubtless belonged to Olympias, Philip's royal wife.

There is a rounded gold head-band, which is adjustable, and the head of a satyr, also in gold, with its head-dress awry. There are two items which are of supreme interest for Macedonia, one of gold and the other of iron. The iron piece is a Macedonian helmet, the first ever to be found in Macedonia made of iron, in the Macedonian design, and is therefore of incomparable value to the archaeologists; and the gold piece is a tripod, like those awarded to winners at the Olympic Games, of the fifth century BC, which has lion's feet with claws, typical of workmanship of the Archaic period. There is an inscription on this tripod, in ancient Greek which is proof of its date, stating that it was a prize for Games in Argos; and its dating would assume it to be a prize awarded to Alexander I of Macedonia, who proved his Argive descent before the Council of the Olympic Games in the early fifth century, and was therefore allowed to compete. He was king of Macedonia from approximately 495–450 BC, and was admitted as an Hellene to the Games at Olympia for his help to the Athenians against the Persians. He was also the first king of Macedonia to introduce Greek ways and customs to the court at Aegea, and invited the poet Pindar to visit him there. Pindar subsequently wrote poems in praise of the king, and also of parts of Macedonia such as Abdera.

The tripod, which was obviously of great importance to the royal house, had doubtless been handed down to Philip; and owing to Alexander the Great's almost permanent absence abroad was buried in Philip's tomb for safe-keeping.

It is as yet too early to assess these remarkable finds from Virgina at their true value, but unquestionably when the scholars and others concerned have worked on and studied all that has been found – and possibly more that will be found during the coming seasons – a considerably amplified page of history, containing much that was hitherto unknown and unproven, will be written for 'proud-voiced Macedonia'. Truly this is her spoil.

Glossary

KRATER	large jar in which water was mixed with wine at mealtimes
THEOROI	religious envoys, or messengers, 'observers'
HEGEMON	leader or ruler
AMPHORA	wine jar
POROS	type of soft stone, much used in building throughout Greece
BASILIKOS	pre-Christian meaning – royal residence
PELIKE	2-handled krater-type jar
THYRSOS	giant fennel stem decorated with ivy
KAUSIA	Macedonian hat
POLIS	'city – state'
KOUROS	nude male sculptured figure
KERYKEION	herald's staff
CHITON	tunic
THIASOS	maenads and satyrs – followers of Dionysos, the 'revel rout'
PETASOS	broad hat normally worn by Greek travellers

Early Helladic period	2500–1900 BC
Middle Helladic period	1900–1660 BC
Mycenaean period	1400–1200 BC
Archaic period	720–480 BC
Classical period	480–323 BC
Hellenistic period	323–27 BC

Bibliography

Andronicos, Manolis, *Greek Museums*
—*Vergina*
Cambridge Ancient History, Vol. VI
Classical Dictionary
Cook, R. M., *Greek Painted Pottery*
Charbonneaux-Villard-Martin, *Classical Greek Art*
Dakaris, S., *The Sanctuary of Dodona*
Ecoles Française d'Athènes, *Guide de Thasos*
Euripides, Translation – William Arrowsmith
Gardiner, Sir Alan, *Egypt of the Pharaohs*
Glover, *Pericles to Philip*
Hammond, N. G. L., *A History of Greece*
Herodotus, *The Histories*
Hesiod, *Theogony, Works and Days*
Homer, *Homeric Hymns*
—*Iliad*
—*Odyssey*
Kirk, G. S., *The Nature of Greek Myths*
Lesky, Albin, *Greek Tragedy*
Pausanias, *Guide to Greece*
Rose, H. J., *Handbook of Greek Mythology*
Thucydides, *The Pelopponesian War*
Wynne-Thomas, J. L., *Legacy of Thasos*

For all reports of recent excavations, publications, etc., the *Journal of Hellenic Studies* has been used.